# Paraguay

## Corruption, Reform, and the Financial System

Jeffrey Franks, Valerie Mercer-Blackman,
Randa Sab, and Roberto Benelli

International Monetary Fund
Washington, DC

©2005 International Monetary Fund

Production: IMF Multimedia Services Division
Typesetting: Alicia Etchebarne-Bourdin
Cover Design: Lai Oy Louie
Photo Credit: Jorge Saenz/AP Photo


**Cataloging-In-Publication Data**

Paraguay : corruption, reform, and the financial system / Jeffrey Franks . . . [et al] — [Washington,
   D.C. : International Monetary Fund, 2005]

   p.  cm.

Includes bibliographical references.
ISBN 1-58906-420-8

   1.  Paraguay — Economic conditions — Statistics. 2. Financial crises — Paraguay. 3. Foreign
exchange rates — Paraguay. I. Franks, Jeffrey R. II. International Monetary Fund.
HC222.P37  2005

The views expressed in this work are those of the authors and do not necessarily represent those of the IMF or IMF policy. The IMF has not edited this publication. Some documents cited in this work may not be available publicly.

Price: $25.00

Please send orders to:
International Monetary Fund, Publication Services
700 19th Street, NW, Washington, DC 20431, U.S.A.
Telephone: (202) 623-7430        Telefax: (202) 623-7201
Internet: http://www.imf.org

# Contents

**Figures**

**Tables**

# Abbreviations

| | |
|---|---|
| BACE | Bayesian averaging of classical estimates |
| BCP | Central Bank of Paraguay |
| BNF | Public development bank |
| CAR | Capital adequacy ratio |
| CIRD | Centro de Información y Recursos para el Desarrollo |
| CPI | Consumer price index |
| DMS | Doppelhoffer, Miller, and Sala-i-Martin |
| DW | Durbin-Watson |
| ECM | Error correction model |
| FSAP | Financial system assessment program |
| GDP | Gross domestic product |
| GNI | Gross national income |
| HP | Hodrick-Prescott |
| IDB | Inter-American Development Bank |
| INCOOP | Supervisory authority of the cooperatives |
| IPS | Social security institute |
| LRM | Central bank bills |
| N | Number of observations |
| NPL | Nonperforming loan |
| OLS | Ordinary least squares |
| REER | Real effective exchange rate |
| ROA | Returns on assets |
| ROE | Returns on equity |
| SIC | Schwartz criterion |
| TFP | Total factor productivity |
| TOT | Terms of trade |
| VAR | Vector autoregression |
| VAT | Value-Added Tax |
| VECM | Vector error correction model |

# Preface

The material presented in this Special Issue was originally prepared as background for discussion at the IMF Executive Board. The authors are grateful to the Paraguayan authorities for extensive discussions and comments and for their assistance in providing data and other source material.

This Special Issue has benefited from the comments of staff in the IMF Western Hemisphere Department and Monetary and Financial Systems Department. The authors appreciate the excellent research assistance provided by Gustavo Ramirez and the outstanding secretarial support provided by Joan McLeod-Tillman and Patricia Delgado Pino. Sean M. Culhane of the External Relations Department coordinated the production of this publication. Alicia Etchebarne-Bourdin of the External Relations Department revised and composed the manuscript.

The opinions expressed are solely those of the authors and do not necessarily reflect the views of the IMF, its Executive Directors, or the Paraguayan authorities.

# Overview

After years of economic stagnation and periodic economic crises, the government of President Nicanor Duarte Frutos took office in August 2003 and embarked on an ambitious program of economic reforms. The new administration agreed on a set of policies to be supported by a Fund arrangement and signed a 15-month Stand-By Arrangement on December 15, 2003.

The authorities adopted a comprehensive program of fiscal and structural reforms to set Paraguay on a path of sustainable growth. The strategy centered on restoring fiscal sustainability, improving the efficiency of the public sector, strengthening the banking sector, improving governance, and fighting corruption. Specifically, they adopted a comprehensive and balanced fiscal package, including measures to increase tax revenues and appropriate spending restraint, as well as efforts to correct financial problems in certain public enterprises. They also reformed the public employees' pension plan. The monetary policy had responded pragmatically to the difficulties faced in 2002.

The Paraguayan economy is emerging from a long period of slow growth. Over the two decades before 2002, per capita income fell by an average of 0.6 percent per year. This stagnation reflected weak macroeconomic management and a series of structural problems, which impeded growth and left the country more vulnerable to the effects of economic shocks. The main structural problems include:

- Political instability. During the 1990s, the political system was rocked by a coup attempt, the assassination of a vice-president, the resignation of a president, and a subsequent period of government by an interim president, González Macchi, who was not popularly elected.

- Serious governance problems. Corruption, inefficiency, poor guarantees of property rights, and lack of transparency have afflicted both the public and private sectors. Paraguay has consistently ranked among the worst in the world in surveys of perception of corruption.

- A weak banking system plagued by a series of crises. Bank closures affected the financial sector in several rounds from 1995 to 2003, reducing the total number of banks from 35 to 14.

- Inefficient public enterprises in key sectors. Government firms are a strong presence in the water, electricity, transport, telecommunications, petroleum, cement, and banking sectors. Many are poorly run, and their performance has depressed growth in the rest of the economy.

- Low and falling productivity. Poor human capital formation, inefficient public services, and governance problems have contributed to the deterioration.

- High poverty and unemployment with limited social protection. Income inequality is high, and nearly half the population lives on less than US$2 per day. Social spending per capita is one-fourth of the Latin American average.

A sharp recession in 2002 was followed by a recovery in 2003 and 2004. The regional crisis, problems with drought and foot-and-mouth disease in agriculture, and a banking crisis all contributed to a drop of 2.3 percent in GDP in 2002. There was a sharp depreciation of the exchange rate in 2002, and inflation accelerated, reaching 20 percent in early 2003. A bumper harvest produced positive GDP growth of an estimated 2.6 percent in 2003. The easing of the regional crisis and the clear victory of Nicanor Duarte Frutos in the April 2003 presidential elections provided an increased perception of economic and political stability later in the year. Banking system deposits recovered, the exchange rate appreciated against the dollar, and inflation eased to 9 percent at year's end. The nonagricultural economy remained stagnant, however. In 2004, the economy continued its recovery and, despite a drought that affected soy, the largest export crop, the economy grew by almost 3 percent, significantly above the average in the past 10 years.

The political environment for reform has improved. President Duarte Frutos has demonstrated an ability to advance important political and economic reforms, despite not having a majority in the Senate. He has appointed reform-minded people to key positions in the government and retains a high degree of support in public opinion polls. However, the government's support in Congress is fragile, with opposition parties often inclined to oppose government initiatives for political reasons and increasing resistance from special interests whose privileges are affected by reform measures. There is also pressure from within the president's own Colorado Party from factions, which have traditionally benefited from patronage and rent-seeking behaviors. Reform efforts must also confront long-standing and pervasive governance problems that seriously affect the efficiency of the public sector and generally act to undermine change. Against this background, Chapter 1 examines how corruption in Paraguay contributed to slow economic growth.

Monetary policy has been geared toward a flexible exchange rate regime since the de facto currency peg was abandoned in 2001. The Central Bank of Paraguay (BCP) has limited the growth of the domestic money supply mainly through sales of the bank's *Letras de Regulación Monetaria* (LRMs), the stock of which has grown sharply over the past three years, from PARG 300 billion at end-2001 to around PARG 1.6 trillion in mid-2004. Interest rates on LRMs have declined from their peak of 33 percent in August 2002, reaching 9½ percent by April 2004. Base money growth accelerated sharply in 2003 as the economy began to remonetize after the banking crises. The appreciation of the *guaraní* in 2003 also contributed to a greater willingness of agents to hold local currency, and, as a result, some de-dollarization occurred (from 69 percent of deposits at end-2002 to 64 percent in mid-2004).

The financial system has improved, but weaknesses persist. In 2003, deposits largely recovered from the sharp drop in the 2002 banking crisis, and they continued to rise in 2004. Credit to the private sector, in contrast, has continued to fall, down by 4 percent in May 2004. Higher deposits and falling credit has left banks in a highly liquid position. Much of this excess liquidity has been deposited in the central bank, contributing to the decline in the growth rate of base money. Nonperforming loan (NPL) ratios have begun to decline, although—at 13 percent for private banks—they remain high, while provisioning requirements are still low. Profitability of the banking system remains low, with several banks continuing to produce losses. Several banks have also closed or reduced significantly their operations in Paraguay over the past two years. Chapter 2 examines the impact of the financial crises on private sector credit.

The fiscal situation has improved markedly since the new government took office in August 2003. The consolidated balance of the nonfinancial public sector (NFPS) moved from a deficit of 3.1 percent of GDP in 2002 to balance in 2003 and a higher-than-expected surplus of 2½ percent of GDP in 2004. The primary balance also improved markedly, as interest payments as a percent of GDP stabilized, owing to the sharp reduction in debt-service payments arrears and low international interest rates. The main features of the improvements in 2003 were (1) expenditures were tightly controlled throughout the year in the central government, and (2) tax collections increased sharply beginning in August 2003, owing to leadership changes in tax and customs administrations. And the recovery of the exchange rate from the steep decline in 2002 contributed to an improvement of public enterprises' outlook. In the medium term, the public finances are expected to improve further. The approval of the Public Pension Reform Law (the *caja fiscal*) is expected to generate savings on the order of ½ percent of GDP in transfer payments. Chapter 3 assesses the reform of the caja fiscal.

During 2003, the guaraní appreciated by 13 percent against the dollar. The general decline of the dollar in the world left the appreciation of the guaraní in real effective terms at 9.5 percent. In the first half of 2004, the currency appreciated somewhat further, despite central bank intervention. However, after the depreciation experienced by the economy in 2001 and 2002, the guaraní does not appear overappreciated in real terms when the fundamentals of the economy are taken into account. Chapter 4 estimates the long-term equilibrium real exchange rate at the end of 2003 and the misalignment in the real exchange rate.

Structural reform remained a key priority in the government's program. The government has reformed the public sector pension system and has begun to develop a reform plan for the civil service. A census of employees has been conducted to detect phantom workers and those collecting double salaries. The authorities have taken measures to improve transparency and governance in Paraguay. The passage of the Fiscal Adjustment Law, with its elimination of tax loopholes and strengthened tax administration, will reduce corruption in the tax system. The approval of the new customs code should reduce corruption associated with international trade and smuggling. The code grants operational and financial autonomy to customs and greatly expands its powers of investigation and enforcement. In addition, efforts are being made to improve transparency. Independent audits of numerous public entities are under way. The procurement reform approved by Congress in 2002 is fully functioning for all public sector agencies. Purchases must be made through a public web-based bidding process. Some entities are already reporting significant savings in procurement costs. In the financial sector, the Bank Superintendency has made progress in applying new supervisory requirements, and implementation of the new bank resolution law has begun, with the deposit guarantee fund operating.

# 1

# Has Corruption in Paraguay Contributed to Slow Economic Growth?

## A. Introduction

Paraguay has long-standing problems with corruption and contraband. It figures as the most corrupt country in Latin America and the third most corrupt out of 133 countries, according to the 2003 Transparency International *Corruption Perception Index*. Various articles and surveys report evidence of widespread contraband.[1] Paraguay scores third from last out of 125 countries in the Economist Intelligence Unit country risk rating for investors, in particular owing to its low score on political effectiveness.[2] The World Bank's Governance Indicators 2002[3] show Paraguay particularly low in the subcategories of "government effectiveness" (the capacity of the government to manage resources effectively) and "control of corruption" (the degree of compliance with rules by citizens and the state) (Table 1.1).

This chapter will explore to what extent these endemic governance problems have affected economic growth. With the exception of a favorable period between 1962 and 1981, Paraguay has not been a fast grower. The average per capita growth rate since 1938 has been 1.1 percent. While much of Latin America recouped the output decline of the "lost decade" of the 1980s, Paraguay's per capita GDP continued to decline (by an average of 0.6 percent per year in the two decades before 2002).

---

[1]See reports by Sciscioli (2003), Smith (2003), Tobar (2002), and U.S. Department of Commerce (1999).

[2]Economist Intelligence Unit (2003).

[3]Kaufmann, Kraay, and Mastruzzi (2003). The 2002 indicator included 195 countries.

### Table 1.1. World Bank's Governance Indicators for Paraguay

| Governance Indicator | Percentile Rank, 1998 | Percentile Rank, 2002 | Latin America and the Caribbean, 2002 | Number of Surveys/Polls |
|---|---|---|---|---|
| Voice and accountability | 41 | 32 | 61 | 4 |
| Political stability/ no violence | 35 | 15 | 51 | 4 |
| Government effectiveness | 9 | 7 | 53 | 4 |
| Regulatory quality | 35 | 31 | 58 | 3 |
| Rule of law | 23 | 12 | 53 | 6 |
| Control of corruption | 9 | 4 | 55 | 5 |

Sources: Kaufmann, Kraay, and Mastruzzi (2003); and Governance Indicators (2002).

Recent empirical research has shown that good governance and low corruption are highly correlated to per capita income (Figure 1.1). However, this simple relationship is just the manifestation of complicated underlying factors. Research on corruption and growth has focused on the channels through which corruption creates a large disincentive for productive investment and economic growth. However, cross-country growth studies that have conducted rigorous robustness tests (in particular Levine and Renelt, 1992; Sala-i-Martin, 1997; and Doppelhoffer, Miller, and Sala-i-Martin, 2000) do not find that the standard indicators of corruption or lack of political rights (which affect government effectiveness) have a direct effect on economic growth after controlling for other factors, and Barro (1999) shows that electoral democracies have not necessarily grown faster than dictatorships during the postwar era. Indeed, Paraguay's growth in the 1970s was the highest in Latin America, at the height of Alfredo Stroessner's dictatorship. Conversely, GDP growth in the 1990s was one of the lowest in the region.

This chapter will argue that both corruption and low output growth were caused primarily by weak institutionalism, which has persisted throughout most of Paraguay's history. The direct causality is not from corruption to growth, as corruption is not a significant variable in econometric estimates once we control for other standard growth determinants. Instead, low growth and corruption are jointly determined by various outcomes that resulted from the weak institutional quality. In turn, the institutions in Paraguay were shaped by a politico-economic and historical process, and it was the weakness of these institutions that bred corruption.

Following some historical background, the chapter describes how corruption is manifested in Paraguay. The chapter distinguishes between factors that explain the growth performance of Paraguay since 1960 (where corruption does not directly enter as a significant factor) and factors that explain the relative level of income of Paraguay in the past 40 or 50 years compared with other countries.

**Figure 1.1. Relationship Between GDP per Capita and Corruption**

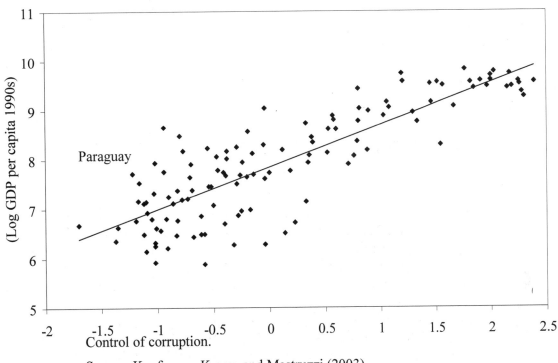

Source: Kaufmann, Kraay, and Mastruzzi (2003).

Measured from the viewpoint of institutional development, 40 years could be considered a relatively short period. Indeed, recent seminal research on the subject has shown that institutional quality and corruption levels are important determinants of the level of per capita income today, as well as 40 years ago. The chapter then illustrates, via a reduced-form version of a politico-economy model by Acemoglu (2003), how Paraguay's weak institutions may have led to long-term growth below its potential. Finally, we briefly consider how Paraguay could improve its institutional process. To the extent that prudent policies and the opening up to the international rules of the game will exert pressure for changes in the economic power base, a gradual improvement of institutional quality will ensue, which is necessary for sustained long-run growth.

The chapter is divided as follows. Section B describes the sources of corruption in Paraguay in a historical context. Section C looks at the determinants of growth in Paraguay, extrapolating from recent cross-country empirical work. Section D considers recent research on corruption and growth. Section E describes how a model by Acemoglu aptly depicts the processes that led to a low-quality institutional base in Paraguay and thus low growth, and considers how better policies in Paraguay could lead to sustainable growth. Section F concludes.

## B. Corruption in Paraguay

Corruption is the manifestation of a weak institutional base, where institutions could be broadly defined as the organization of society, or the de facto rules of the game in the economic, political, and social spheres. To understand how the institutions of Paraguay came about, it is important to look at the historical context. Much of its history was similar to that of other countries of the region; here we focus on what was unique to Paraguay.

### Historical roots

Historically, Paraguay has held together through a cohesive system of informality, always susceptible to the political and economic stability of its two large neighbors, Argentina and Brazil. Without access to the sea, Paraguay was forced to maintain a delicate diplomatic balance between the two countries, while distinguishing itself through a strong national identity.[4] When the balance was not maintained or there was regional instability, the consequences were devastating. When President Solano Lopez declared war on Argentina, Brazil, and Uruguay in 1865, a brutal five-year conflict started—The Triple Alliance War, which left Paraguay poverty-stricken, after losing 75 percent of its population and making large concessions to its victors. As some recent research has suggested (see Section D, below), the fact that Paraguay was landlocked by itself did not hinder its development. Its relationship with its neighbors, which affected its access to the sea, became one of the most important factors in shaping its institutions.

The intentions of the groups in power in Paraguay determined the nature of institution building. The mode of colonization in Paraguay before independence has been characterized by historians as extractive, as the Spaniards showed little interest in settling and building high-quality institutions, which may have compromised the establishment of solid property rights and the rule of law.[5] These settlements contrast with the Jesuit settlements in the mid-1700s in Paraguay, which were well organized, democratic, and highly productive missions until their disappearance shortly after 1767.[6] Even after independence, following

---

[4]This is manifested through the guaraní language, which, even to date, is spoken by more than 80 percent of Paraguayans.

[5]See for example Engermann and Sokoloff (1994) and Acemoglu, Johnson, and Robinson (2001).

[6]The Jesuits settled in what is now the southeastern part of Paraguay, as well as in southwestern Brazil and northeastern Argentina. The society was then principally concerned with improving its well-being and protecting property rights. King Carlos III expelled the Jesuits from the Spanish colonies, and shortly thereafter the missions lost their value, became badly administered, and were eventually abandoned by the guaraníes. See Baruja, Perez Paiva, and Pinto Schaffroth (2003, Chapter 3).

the Triple Alliance War, the Brazilians and Argentines sent to administer the country in shambles granted themselves prized pieces of land and joined the elite to follow a relatively extractive policy thereafter.[7] Since then, Paraguay became, and continues to be, an oligarchic society with the political and economic power in the hands of a few leaders. Until fairly recently, the government continued to shift back and forth between unelected military governments of the two rival political parties: the Liberal Party and the Colorado Party.

Between 1904 and 1936 the Liberal Party governed the country, a period characterized by extreme instability in governance (there were 22 presidents in total), thus setting the stage for the consolidation of the power of the executive branch starting in 1940. Policymaking was conducted by a fractionalized political oligarchy with low administrative competence, and corruption weakened the capacity of the state to deliver services. Ironically, Paraguay's victory over Bolivia in the 1935 Chaco War led to protests by the population, particularly veterans, about the worsening social conditions at home. The liberals thus briefly lost power to the Febrerista Party, headed by the Argentine colonel Franco. However, Franco was unable to deliver land reforms for fear of expropriating powerful landowners, many Argentines, and soon the military gained back the power for the Liberal Party. In its quest for a strong and credible leader, in 1939 the Liberal Party chose General Estigarribia as their presidential candidate, a war hero who had led Paraguay to victory in the Chaco War. Estigarribia gave himself temporary dictatorial powers as he aggressively pursued reforms. A plebiscite by a population hungry for order ratified the constitution of 1940, which disproportionately expanded the power of the executive branch. To some extent this set the stage for partly legitimizing the dictatorships that would follow.

The art of rent seeking became highly developed during the dictatorship of Stroessner (1954–89), an era when resources were channeled to Colorado Party interests.[8] Party loyalists were made the main administrators of the government regardless of their competence. The power network was so tight that there was no distinction among the party, the military government, and the public sector. Most businesspeople who showed their allegiance to the regime could operate unrestricted and with complete impunity, while most activities outside of the power group's control, including investments, were repressed.[9] In the 1970s, the border town of Ciudad del Este, the hub of high-growth activities, developed as an almost anarchic frontier where large-scale smuggling, counterfeiting, arms

---

[7]See Baruja, Perez Paiva, and Pinto Schaffroth (2003) for an excellent recount.

[8]As discussed in World Bank (1996, Chapter 1).

[9]See World Bank (2003b). Also based on conversations with Pilar Callizo from the organization *Transparency Paraguay*.

trading, and narco-traffic coexisted side by side without restrictions.[10] Public investment projects in Paraguay, including those built in the 1990s, consisted of large-scale infrastructure projects (the largest being the binational Itaipú and Yacyretá dams). There were numerous reports of diverted and misused funds, as well as the use of the state by those involved in the contracts to enrich themselves.[11] To this day, the Yacyretá hydroelectric dam, built jointly with Argentina, is known in the region as "a monument to corruption,"[12] barely finished and facing serious legal and financial problems.

The remnants of Paraguay's past still influence the socioeconomic structure today. The high level of informality that was inherited from the Stroessner era, defined in this context as a form of decision making that is highly discretionary, confined to a tight group of loyalists, and lacking in legal documentation, remains prevalent in many areas. Moreover, the perceptions of informality related to corruption remain: a 2002 study by the Centro de Información y Recursos para el Desarrollo (CIRD) showed that people still believed organized crime had almost as much power as the central government, as "they are allowed to conduct their business of contraband and delinquency with total impunity."[13]

The weak institutional base Paraguay faces is particularly acute in four areas, to be discussed below. These are (1) the judicial system, (2) tax and customs administration, (3) government expenditures, and (4) patronage in the public sector. As will be noted, the government that took office in August 2003 has taken serious measures to combat these corrupt forces by taking the first important steps toward improving accountability and transparency of the public institutions.

## The judicial system

Various studies have shown that the judiciary has been mired by political influence and has therefore been unable to enforce property rights. The 2003 *Index of Economic Freedom* (Heritage Foundation, 2003) gives Paraguay the lowest score in terms of enforcement of property rights, citing a U.S. Commerce Department report that noted, "Judges are often pressured by politicians and other persons whose interests are at stake." It also noted that "there is little confidence in the legal system because cases routinely take several years, even as

---

[10]See for example Arfield (2002) and United States Commerce Department (1999). It is noteworthy that many of the main businesses in Ciudad del Este were not run by native Paraguayans but by Brazilians or non-Paraguayans who may have had legitimate businesses elsewhere.

[11]See Baruja, Perez Paiva, and Pinto Schaffroth (2003) and Sciscioli (2003) for recent prominent examples.

[12]Term used in various local newspaper articles.

[13]Centro de Información y Recursos para el Desarrollo (2002). Information taken from World Bank (2003b).

long as a decade, to resolve, and because accusations of undue influence on judges are widespread." The CIRD study showed that less that 1 percent of the population believed the judiciary was not corrupt.

Challenges to laws almost always prevail, thus making new laws difficult to apply and existing laws difficult to enforce. There are numerous laws in Paraguay, which tend to be long and sometimes contradictory. This aspect can make the application of the laws susceptible to the discretion of the judges, who can choose which law will prevail in a particular case. Public prosecutors are "inexperienced, understaffed, and function without basic equipment such as telephones and faxes,"[14] and in general judges and prosecutors are not well remunerated and thus are more susceptible to bribes. It has been almost impossible for the Paraguayan government to prevail when firing a civil servant or prosecuting a tax evader. For example, the Civil Service Law, passed in 2000, which placed more responsibility on civil servants to perform, has been mired by suits of unconstitutionality and is effectively inactive (the current civil service legislation contains no principles of ethical conduct for public officials). Suits of unconstitutionality continue to be filed disputing the 2003 Public Pension Reform Law, which restricted highly generous pension benefits for civil servants. The precedent has been that the challengers always won, however unreasonable the suit.[15] The state typically ended up paying more in legal compensation than it saved by withdrawing unearned benefits. In the case of prosecuting or fining tax evaders, the process took years and gave rise to high legal costs, so there was no incentive to prosecute.[16]

The protection of property rights is very difficult, as the lack of a property registry makes claims of land difficult to prove, so the ultimate decisions are made in a political contest. Expropriation of land is still possible in Paraguay,[17] as increasing pressure by peasants for land has led to the invasion of rural properties. The invaded landowner typically takes his or her case to the highest levels of government, with settlement of the case consisting of the state purchasing the land—sometimes at inflated prices—and giving it to the invaders.[18] The state therefore bears the cost, channeling its scarce resources to outside activities, while creating incentives for continued land invasions and deterring potential investors who see no guarantee of property rights.

---

[14]World Bank (2003a, p. 5).

[15]Based on conversations with officials at the Paraguayan Ministry of Finance.

[16]See World Bank (2003a).

[17]See U.S. Department of Commerce (2002).

[18]Various stories of these land invasions have appeared recently. See for example "Amenaza de Invasiones Sigue Latente," 2004 *Diario ABC,* Asunción, July 18.

The replacement of six of the nine Supreme Court justices in early 2004 was the first effort to attack this large source of corruption, and the move was widely supported by the population. This action was necessary for restoring the rule of law and creating an environment for renewed investment. Appointees should be chosen for their qualifications rather than their party affiliation.

## Tax and customs administration

Until mid-2004, the tax system suffered from major deficiencies in the form of multiple tax exemptions (included in 42 separate laws), which not only caused a revenue loss but also created opportunities for tax evasion and corruption. Most studies, including Paraguayan official reports, estimate Value-Added Tax (VAT) evasion at 45–60 percent.[19] A large problem with tax collection was the high level of corruption in the tax collection institutions themselves. Most officials owed their positions to patronage regardless of their ability to perform the duties, with minimum training and very low remuneration. In customs, there were networks of corruption composed of customs officials in partnership with members of Congress, dispatchers, and importers, who retained large parts of tax revenues for themselves.[20]

One measure of the extent of institutions' corruption is the increase in revenues that has resulted from the recent high-level appointments to the tax and customs administrations of competent officials known for their integrity. In September 2003, these administrators proceeded to close customs checkpoints and place tax officials and auditors suspected of corruption on leave with pay. This seemingly simple measure accounted for most of the 40 percent increase in tax and customs revenue for almost a year thereafter, in part because the organized corruption networks were ruptured, and in part because the tax authority gained more credibility with the public and was no longer considered an ally of the corrupt networks. The current administrators have stated that part of their daily work consists of keeping away individuals offering bribes.

## Government expenditures

Government spending in Paraguay has been characterized as a vehicle for channeling resources to government loyalists, rather than as the use of funds for the provision of public services.[21] Almost three-fourths of central government

---

[19]See in particular IMF (1999).

[20]See Paraguayan newspaper reports: "Denuncian que Sigue Vigente en Hacienda el Famoso Maletín," 2004b *Diario ABC,* Asunción, July 16; "Faltante Detectado en Aduana ya Llega a Casi G4,000 millones," 2004b *Diario ABC,* Asunción, May 26, 2004).

[21]See World Bank (1996).

current expenditures go to civil servants' salaries or pensions. Until recently, they all had to be Colorado Party members. Until late 2003, public procurement in Paraguay was governed by outdated, rigid, and cumbersome legislation. The process of awarding contracts was so nontransparent that there were frequent cases of cost overruns and phantom subcontractors who submitted false bills.[22] A World Bank (2003b) governance diagnosis survey in 2000 found that contractors and suppliers who did not do business with the state cited the following reasons: (1) requests for bribes from public employees (62 percent), (2) the complexity of the contracting processes (47 percent), (3) lack of government contacts that would give them access to new contracts (37 percent), and (4) the high cost of participation (33 percent).

The budget process in Paraguay in the past has been characterized as highly discretionary and driven by political favoritism. The final allocation of funds across ministries or entities used to be largely a function of the political influence of the minister or regional leader, rather than the economic and social benefits of the specific projects. In the past it was common for the executive branch and Congress to inflate the tax revenue projections in the budget to unrealistic figures to increase simultaneously certain expenditure lines without having to propose compensatory cuts.[23]

Traditionally, there was low accountability regarding funds transferred to the rest of the public sector.[24] The scope of internal and external audits was limited, and it was rare for anyone to be held accountable. In practice, there is a complete lack of clarity regarding the responsibilities of subnational governments and some discretionary authority over transfers received from the central government. The few regulatory entities that receive funds are not independent of the executive branch. Moreover, the public banks are mired in nonperforming loans, owing to a tradition of offering lines of credit to preferred sectors that do not repay,[25] as well as highly subsidized mortgages and personal lines of credit to their employees.

### Patronage in government

Paraguayan public institutions were traditionally shaped by groups that "have finely developed the art of rent-seeking. The base of the system is the patronage

---

[22]See the 2003 ABC news report on a recent Madame Lynch road project, "Desnudan Graves Irregularidades en Manejos de Proyectos de MOPC," *ABC News*, Asunción, December 23.

[23]World Bank (2003b, p. 38).

[24]See IMF (2003).

[25]See for example "Empresa con Deuda 'Pesada' en el BNF Son Urgidas a Pagar," 2004 *Diario ABC*, Asunción, April 27; article on Banco Nacional del Fomento (BNF).

politics of the Colorado party, which would 'nominate' party faithfuls to public institutions."[26] Although there are now three parties with more or less equal representation in Congress, the culture of decision making still works on a very informal basis. A 2002 study described the political parties, which "once in government, would make the state a prize to be distributed through clientelism."[27] Public institutions were largely formed by patronage jobs, many of which lacked a civil service career ladder. It was commonly accepted that "whoever came to power would "'return favors'" by granting employment and or/benefits to their supporters, family and friends."[28] Until recently, a large group of individuals would be hired with an incoming administration and placed on the payroll without a job description or a function, let alone qualifications.[29] There is no meritocratic system of promotions.[30] Organized groups rose within the ranks of the institutions to channel money either to the Colorado Party or as a payoff for employment.[31, 32]

It is important to note that Paraguayans are not innately corrupt, but that institutions were weakened to such a degree by the historical circumstances, as mentioned earlier, that the benefits from partaking in the established corrupt system outweighed the costs of not doing so. Many officials under a different institutional environment may have remained honest and performed their jobs, but under such an environment it was clearly more beneficial for most to go along with—or even partake in—the rent-seeking activities.[33] Moreover, the ruling political classes had no incentive to give up their power base and change the status quo because there was no benefit for them. The following section looks at the factors that determined GDP growth in Paraguay since 1960.

---

[26]World Bank (2003a, p. 4).

[27]Prats (2002).

[28]See World Bank (2003b, p. 34).

[29]In some public enterprises there are cases of people not showing up to work for months at a time while remaining on the payroll. See World Bank (2003b).

[30]Even in the central bank, one of the best-run public institutions in Paraguay, pay is based on the highest professional level ever reached, not on the functions of a post. Some technical professionals choose to work as drivers but continue to receive the salary of a technical professional.

[31]The conclusion of the CIRD study (cited in footnote 13) was that "it is ominous for democratic governance that most of the public believes that the State is controlled or infiltrated by an association dedicated to crime and illegality and there is no action with respect to this."

[32]In late 2003, the president of the Social Security Institute (IPS) was replaced with a technically competent administrator who uncovered small organized crime groups operating within the institution. The new IPS president noted that these mafias had created parallel, undocumented accounting systems to siphon funds to their respective groups.

[33]This situation is widely described in the economic literature of corruption (see Mauro, 2004; and Schleifer and Vishny, 1993). Once the institutional system crosses a threshold where a critical mass of people are involved in the corruption, the penalty for being punished becomes minimal compared with the gains from partaking in the corruption and it becomes a vicious cycle difficult to break.

## C. Growth in Paraguay

Paraguay's per capita real GDP over the past 65 years (since 1938) has grown by 1.1 percent per year on average, with a surge of growth in the 1960s and 1970s followed by a declining trend starting in 1981 (Figure 1.2). The main growth activities consisted of reexporting business to neighboring countries (so-called "triangular trade"), small cotton cultivations, and public sector employment. Since 1982 per capita output has declined by an average of 0.6 percent per year.

The sources of growth during the high-growth period of 1961–81 came from activities that would become unsustainable with globalization. A large part of the growth in the 1960s and 1970s followed the prosperity of the region. However, growth in the 1970s was particularly high in Paraguay, fueled by smuggling (which took advantage of the protectionist trade policies of Brazil and Argentina), as well as the initiation of the Itaipú dam construction, which increased gross capital formation almost 10 percentage points of GDP between 1970 and 1975. The Itaipú project has been generally beneficial to Paraguay; however, it was a one-time investment project with little or no transfer of technology to the rest of the economy. Thereafter, growth through smuggling became unsustainable as average tariffs fell in neighboring countries. Triangular trade, in particular, has fallen significantly as a result of the successful implementation of the *Mercosur* free-trade agreement and greater border controls. This and the underlying structural weaknesses led to an exhaustion of Paraguay's economic paradigm in the 1980s and 1990s.

The still-large domestic informal sector, a remnant from the past, is one of the main sources of inefficiencies of the economy and is likely contributing negatively to growth. Informal activities account for almost 50 percent of Paraguayan economic activity in trade and services,[34] and consist of mostly small-scale family businesses and commerce intensive in low-skilled labor. To the extent that these activities are less able to take advantage of economies of scale, they are less able to demand the protection of property rights and to attract foreign investment. They also tend to be less productive in new technologies and can result in higher taxes for the formal economy (compared with a system where there are no incentives for informality).[35] An Inter-American Development Bank (IDB) report in 2003 estimated that the high level of

---

[34]See estimates of the informal sector in IMF (2000).

[35]Of course, it is better to have an informal sector that can provide services more efficiently than a corrupt formal sector, than to not have one at all. Indeed, Schleifer and Vishny (1993) characterize the rise of the unofficial sector in any country as the rational response of producers to a system where the formal rules and regulations are de facto nonexistent. The relevant benchmark being used here is a hypothetical situation in which Paraguay were completely formal.

### Figure 1.2. Long-Run per Capita Output Growth

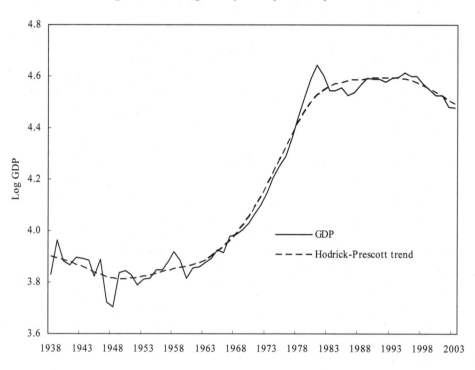

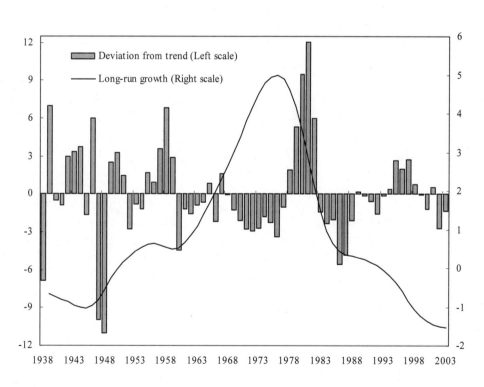

Source: Central Bank of Paraguay; and IMF staff estimates.

informality could generate up to 60 percent lower annual profits for the formal sector in Paraguay as a result of illegitimate competition.[36]

In very recent years large cultivations of soy and other grains, and to a lesser extent cattle-rearing, have proven to be relatively profitable activities. Nonetheless, they currently exist as an enclave with a strong foreign investment component. The narrow tax base and level of informality have prevented the economic benefits of these activities from quickly spreading to other sectors of society.

While capital investment contributed greatly to growth in the 1970s, negative total factor productivity (TFP) explains the decline of output over the past two decades. Figure 1.3 shows the Solow decomposition of output growth in Paraguay taken from Loayza, Fajnzylber, and Calderón (2002), where the estimates are derived using a quality-controlled labor-input variable (adjusted for human capital). TFP contributes negatively to growth, by 3 percent in the 1980s and 1.6 percent in the 1990s. While labor input's contribution to growth has been relatively stable, the contribution of capital to growth declined substantially in the 1990s. However, Paraguay's capital investment has been relatively high since the early 1980s compared with other countries' (ranging between 23 and 25 percent of GDP; see Figure 1.4). This suggests that the negative total factor productivity reflects the very inefficient investments, perhaps in part as a result of the high levels of informality of the economy.

Inefficient infrastructure investment could also explain the very small contribution of capital accumulation to growth in the 1990s. Investment of the general government, which consists of social and physical infrastructure, has been quite small compared with that of other countries (Figure 1.4). Investment by public enterprises has also been small and relatively inefficient, barely covering replacement investment. With the exception of the Itaipú dam, the low levels of infrastructure investment may also be hindering growth: the return to infrastructure investment has been quite high in other South American economies.[37] However, more infrastructure investment does not imply more infrastructure output if the projects are mired with inefficiencies and corruption. Tanzi and Davoodi (1997) have shown how large public investment projects can be associated with corruption: even though the ex-ante return of the project may be high, the ex-post return can be quite low. A notoriously large investment in

---

[36]Report to the incoming president, Nicanor Duarte, July 2003. See also the report, "BID Estima Que el 50 Percent de la Economía es Informal," 2003 *Diario Ultima Hora*, July 16.

[37]A study on growth in World Bank (2003b) cites research that reports GDP elasticities with respect to infrastructure stocks of about 0.15 for Bolivia, Colombia, Mexico, and Venezuela; 0.23 for Argentina; and more than 0.3 for Brazil.

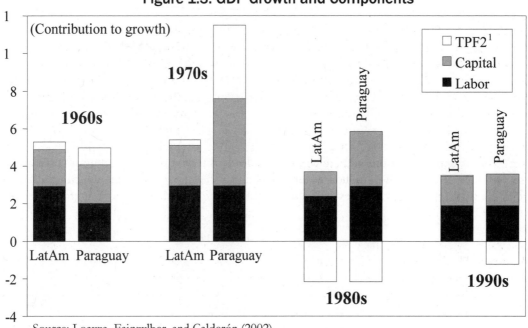

**Figure 1.3. GDP Growth and Components**

Source: Loayza, Fajnzylber, and Calderón (2002).

[1]TFP2 = total factor productivity adjusted by human capital.
[2]LatAm=Latin America.

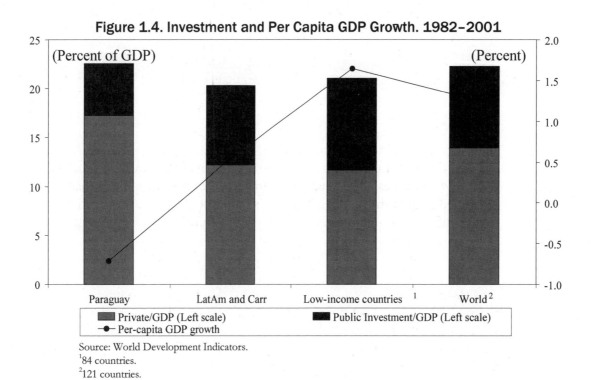

**Figure 1.4. Investment and Per Capita GDP Growth. 1982–2001**

Source: World Development Indicators.

[1]84 countries.
[2]121 countries.

---

> ### Box 1.1. ESSAP Investment Project
>
> ESSAP is responsible for the provision and sanitation of water for about 2.9 million people, most of them in Greater Asunción. It received loans from official sources of roughly US$70 million in the mid-1990s for two large projects. According to the current president of ESSAP, about 50 percent of the funds were spent on auditing and administration of the projects, much higher than what would be warranted. World Bank (1996) noted that this amount was given in the context of past irregularities in the award and control of construction contracts, which had substantially wasted investment funds. The first project consisted of building a water-filtration terminal in a relatively poor and sparsely populated urban area, which already had small wells providing water relatively efficiently. The result was very low-capacity utilization, as there was limited demand from a pool of very poor customers. The second project was a US$20 million water tunnel under the city of Asunción, which was designed to widen the network capacity. However, the feeder tubes were never completed; therefore, there is no way to get the water to the outlying areas, so the tunnel lies idle. ESSAP's debt-service obligations are projected to exceed its net income every year through 2020 as a result of this loan, so the central government, as guarantor, will have to pay the difference. Without this debt ESSAP would have a small surplus. The indebtedness that resulted from this project has made it very difficult for ESSAP to perform maintenance investment, let alone attract badly needed private investment.

the public water and sewage company, ESSAP, in the mid-1990s illustrates how a project with a very high ex-ante rate of return, when mired in inefficiency and irregularities, left Paraguay worse off than without the project (see Box 1.1).

## Cross-country comparisons

Recent research on the determinants of growth across countries has narrowed substantially the set of robust explanatory variables, and governance variables have not generally proven to be robust. Doppelhoffer, Miller, and Sala-i-Martin (2000) (henceforth DMS) recently devised a test of robustness of cross-country growth determinants, the Bayesian Averaging of Classical Estimates (BACE). They construct regression estimates as a weighted average of ordinary least squares (OLS) estimates for every possible combination of included variables on a set of 98 countries. Of 32 standard variables, they find 12 to be partially correlated to growth (i.e., their sign and significance do not change more than 97 percent of the time when other variables are included or excluded). Another five variables are found to be marginally correlated. With regards to variables that may be relevant for the Paraguayan case, DMS finds the real exchange rate distortions variable to be negatively related to income growth but barely making it to the first category. The variable denoting the lack of political rights is marginally correlated to growth. Moreover, DMS find that *government spending to GDP* is important but not particularly robust, as the sign of its coefficient changes for different specifications. Other variables related to corruption and governance are not significant.

A cross-country OLS regression using the most robust specification reported by DMS and using their data set and time period was estimated. The purpose was to consider whether such an equation could explain economic growth in Paraguay. Table 1.2 shows the variable definitions and results using the DMS data set. The variables in equation (1) are the 12 independent variables that passed the BACE test, where the dependant variable is per capita GDP growth between 1960 and 1992 (denoted $Gr$). This regression should give a well-specified equation of the determinants of growth, at least for the countries in the sample and the time period studied. The question is whether the predicted value of the dependant variable for Paraguay (denoted $\hat{Gr}$) varies significantly from the actual value ($Gr$).

Two variables are added to the cross-country regression. Equations (2) and (3) add to this set governance and corruption variables, respectively. Equation (2) includes *PRIGHTSB*, the variable denoting the lack of political rights from the Barro and Lee data set (see DMS), and equation (3) includes in *C.CORRUPTION* a measure of the extent of control of corruption in 2002 (from the *Governance Indicators III* data set; see Kaufmann, Kraay, and Mastruzzi, 2003).

The governance and corruption variables are insignificant, and their inclusion does not contribute to explain Paraguay's growth performance. Equation (1) is a robust and significant equation with all coefficients significant at the 95 percent level, except for the Latin America and the Sub-Saharan Africa dummy variables. The regression predicts Paraguay's average annual per capita GDP growth during the period to be 0.71 percent, whereas the actual value was 1.9 percent. Nonetheless, the difference ($\hat{Gr} - Gr$) is within 1 standard deviation. The coefficient values and significance of the regressions do not change when we include the lack of political rights variable (*PRIGHTSB*) and control of corruption variable (*C.CORRUPTION*). Moreover, the coefficients of the newly included variables are insignificant (less so for the latter), and the predicted values barely differ from those in equation (1) and move in the "wrong" direction: $\hat{Gr} = 0.69$ percent and 0.61 percent, respectively, compared with 0.71 in equation (1). This underprediction of Paraguay's growth rate in cross-country work, at least between 1960 and 1980, has also been found by Loayza, Fajnzylber, and Calderón (2002) in their study of Latin America.

There are three possible and related reasons why the growth equations underpredict Paraguay's growth: exports may have been underestimated, the triangular trade was not accounted for, or the growth spur from unofficial sources in the 1970s could not be explained by the long-run model.

The first possibility is that the variable denoting primary exports to total exports (*PRIEXP70*), which contributed negatively to growth, was de facto much lower during the period considered. Unofficial trade (smuggling) during the 1970s could have been as large as 30 percent of GDP (see IMF, 2000). Since 1995 reexports are still estimated at over 60 percent of total exports, many of these nonagricultural in nature. If a more reliable estimate, which included the

## Table 1.2. Results from the DMS Growth Regressions
### *Dependent Variable: Per Capita GDP Growth 1960–1992 (Gr)*[1]
### *(t-statistics in italics)*

| Equation | (1) | (2) | (3) |
|---|---|---|---|
| C | 5.18 | 5.39 | 5.57 |
| | *5.87* | *5.25* | *5.93* |
| GDP60 | –0.78 | –0.79 | –0.81 |
| | *–5.69* | *–5.63* | *–5.82* |
| Mining | 5.13 | 5.08 | 5.06 |
| | *6.09* | *5.95* | *6.01* |
| YrsOpen | 0.86 | 0.85 | 0.80 |
| | *4.17* | *4.02* | *3.78* |
| CONFUC | 6.79 | 6.88 | 6.82 |
| | *8.23* | *7.99* | *8.29* |
| LIFEE60 | 0.04 | 0.04 | 0.03 |
| | *2.63* | *2.47* | *2.03* |
| PE60 | 0.93 | 0.93 | 0.97 |
| | *2.05* | *2.05* | *2.14* |
| SSAFRICA | –0.06 | –0.05 | –0.09 |
| | *–0.25* | *–0.21* | *–0.39* |
| MUSLIM | 0.49 | 0.49 | 0.45 |
| | *1.86* | *1.87* | *1.73* |
| LAAM | –0.30 | –0.30 | –0.26 |
| | *–1.39* | *–1.4* | *–1.22* |
| PROT | –0.97 | –0.97 | –1.06 |
| | *–3.39* | *–3.37* | *–3.58* |
| PRIEXP70 | –1.39 | –1.37 | –1.29 |
| | *–4.56* | *–4.45* | *–4.08* |
| RERD | –0.004 | –0.004 | –0.004 |
| | *–2.41* | *–2.35* | *–2.07* |
| PRGHTSB | | –0.02 | |
| | | *–0.41* | |
| C. CORRUPTION | | | 0.13 |
| | | | *1.17* |
| Adj. R-sq | 0.858 | 0.856 | 0.859 |
| Standard error of regression | 19.62 | 19.57 | 19.26 |
| Number of observations | 88 | 88 | 88 |
| *Memo item:* | | | |
| $(\hat{Gr}–Gr)$ value for Paraguay | 1.19 | 1.21 | 1,27 |

[1]The dependant variable's mean is 1.106 and the standard deviation is 1.357.

**Variable Definitions (from DMS)**

*C* is a constant

*C. CORRUPTION* is corruption.

*GDP60* is log of GDP per capita in purchasing power parity terms in 1960.

*Mining* is the fraction of GDP in mining (from Hall and Jones, 1996).

*YrsOpen* is the number of years the economy has been open between 1950 and 1994 (index computed by Sachs and Warner, 1995).

*CONFUC* is the fraction of the population that follows the Confucian religion.

*LIFEE60* is the life expectancy in 1960.

*PE60* is the primary school enrollment rate in 1960.

*SSAFRICA* is a dummy for Sub-Saharan Africa.

*MUSLIM* is the fraction of the population that is Muslim.

*LAAM* is the Latin American dummy.

*PROT* is the fraction of the population that is Protestant.

*PRIEXP70* is the fraction of primary exports to total exports in 1970 (Sachs and Warner, 1995 data set).

*RERD* is the measure of the real exchange rate distortions (from Levine and Renelt, 1992).

*PRGHTSB* is lack of political rights.

manufacturing (smuggled) exports were included, the predicted growth rate, $\hat{Gr}$, may have been higher.

Another possibility is that the model specified by DMS is not capturing the profitability from the triangular trade. We note that the value of *YrsOpen* for Paraguay, which captures the degree of openness, is relatively low, even though Paraguay was quite open in the black market. The country took advantage of the very high protectionism of its large neighbors, Brazil and Argentina, during that time, as measured by the trade distortion index[38] of these two countries, making smuggling and reexporting very profitable.

Finally, the very high growth rate observed was transient and not sustainable, given Paraguay's initial income and other characteristics. Because Paraguay's growth model was based largely on more temporary sources of growth during the period studied, this growth pattern was unsustainable and unlikely to persist.[39]

It is not surprising that the governance variables are not significant, since the variables that are important in determining growth to some extent embody the weak institutionalism. In other words, these 12 variables in the regression reflect the politico-economic process and in turn determine the low per capita income levels. The strong negative correlation between corruption and *levels* of income shown in Figure 1.1 does not imply causation. Recent research on the subject has found that the omitted variable from this relationship is the institutional quality (i.e., how well society organizes itself). Indeed, Paraguay's relatively low per capita income and low institutional quality have persisted for almost a century.

The recent literature on determinants of countries' income levels (Hall and Jones, 1999; and Rodrick, Subramanian, and Trebbi, 2002) has distinguished between explaining the level of income of a country and explaining the rate of growth over the past few decades. This literature has found that levels of income are strongly correlated to institutional and geographical factors (for example, the legal system, the form of colonization, access to the sea). Moreover, this relationship has persisted. In other words, most countries that were rich in the 1900s tend to stay rich and vice versa, and their institutions have changed very little. For the few notable exceptions, in particular countries in East Asia, the move from low income to high income has resulted from a very strong process

---

[38]A common trade distortion index is the inverse of the overall trade openness indicator (from Levine and Renelt, 1992). Argentina and Brazil rank fourth and fifth lowest, respectively, from a sample of 51 countries, with values of –13 percent and –11 percent compared with a mean for the sample of countries of 3.1 percent.

[39]Loayza, Fajnzylber, and Calderón (2002) also measure the persistence of growth across decades since 1960, and Paraguay is consistently underpredicted in the 1960s and 1970s, but the model predicts accurately the decades of the 1980s and 1990s.

of transformation and industrialization. The next section surveys more recent research on the subject.

## D. Explanation of Effects of Corruption on Levels of per Capita Income

This section considers how recent literature may shed some light on the relationship between corruption and the level of income in Paraguay. Taken together, the results suggest that the corruption of Paraguay today cannot be explained solely by the policies it failed to pursue over the past few decades, but that the explanation came about through a much longer cumulative historical process.

### *Corruption is persistent and evolves from a system with weak institutions.*

Despite increased awareness by policymakers all over the world of the costs of corruption, it has proven to be remarkably persistent. Mauro (2004) develops a model of strategic complementarities to show how some countries seem to be stuck in a "bad equilibrium" of high corruption, low investment, and low growth, whereas others experience minimal corruption and persistently so. The model develops the idea that when corruption is widespread, it does not make sense for individuals to attempt to fight it, even if everyone is better off were corruption eliminated. By contrast, in bureaucracies that are generally honest, a real threat of punishment deters individual civil servants from behaving dishonestly. Sah (1988) presents a learning model of crime participation in which it is easier to observe how members of one's own group operate, thus illustrating how present behavior is affected by that of past generations. Moreover, in many cross-country studies, indices of corruption or institutional strength available for the past two or three decades have been very stable over time.

### *Corruption is costly.*

Extensive literature, notably by Krueger (1974), and Murphy, Schleifer, and Vishny (1993), has analyzed the relationship between rent-seeking behavior and economic inefficiencies. More recently, empirical studies (such as Kaufmann, Kraay, and Zoido-Lobatón 2002) have used corruption indices and concluded that the economic costs of corruption and weak governance are substantial.

### *The institutions chosen in a society came about as a result of conflict within a political and historical process.*

Several recent politico-economy models have shown how the institutions that were chosen were likely the result of social conflict, which benefited some groups of the economy. It is difficult for those in power as a result of the weak institutions to give this up, even if to do so would be pareto-optimal. This is because there is a time-inconsistency problem: those who would benefit from a better power-sharing system cannot credibly commit ex ante to fully compensate those who give it up because there is no way to enforce such a contract. Engermann and Sokoloff (1994) have emphasized the disadvantageous consequences for institutional development of certain patterns of factor endowments, which engender extreme inequalities and enable the entrenchment of a small group of elites.

*Institutional quality is a strong determinant of per capita income: countries that began with a set of low-quality institutions tend to have relatively lower income.*

Acemoglu, Johnson, and Robinson (2001) present results that show institutions' significant effect on income, that is, that institutional differences explain most of the gap between rich and poor countries. They use mortality rates of colonial settlers as an independent instrument for institutional quality, arguing that settler mortality had an important effect on the type of institutions that were built in lands that were colonized by the main European powers. Additional results from Acemoglu, Johnson, Robinson, and Thaicharoen (2003) show that countries with worse institutions because of historical reasons suffer more volatile output growth, bigger crises, and lower growth. Other seminal economics research (for example, North, 1981; and Hall and Jones, 1996) has pointed out the importance of historical factors in creating institutions where producers' property rights are enforced, which is an essential ingredient for successful long-run economic performance.

*Other factors such as trade openness, while important, do not have as strong a direct effect on the level of income as does institutional quality.*

Some recent literature has emphasized the importance of trade, as well as the importance of geographical factors such as access to the sea, on economic growth (notably Sachs and Warner, 1995). These factors are less important when explaining levels of income. Rodrick, Subramanian, and Trebbi (2002) find that the quality of institutions trumps these other effects. Once institutions are controlled for, trade integration has no direct effect on incomes, while geography has at best weak effects. They find that trade integration (trade openness) has a positive indirect effect on a country's income to the extent that it helps improve institutions, as the coefficients of trade and institutional quality exert a positive impact on each other (i.e., integration can have an indirect effect on incomes via its effects on institutional quality).

## E. Modeling the Political Economy of Growth

The results from the recent literature and the stylized facts of Paraguay's economy indicate the importance of explaining how weak institutionalism over a long period of time can lead to lower-than-potential long-term growth, even though there may temporarily be short spurts of high growth. The results also suggest why a minority group with the economic power will choose to erect high entry barriers over successive generations to maintain the status quo from which it benefits.

The model, presented in detail in the appendix to this chapter, shows the trade-off between a democratic and an oligarchic society. There are two types of agents (productive and nonproductive), and two policy distortions are presented: taxation (which tends to be higher in a democracy) and entry barriers (which tend to be higher in an oligarchy). Taxes at time $t$ ($\tau_t$), which redistribute income from entrepreneurs to workers, are distortionary because they discourage entrepreneurial investment. However, the government uses the proceeds to make transfers to all agents ($T_t$), thereby improving income distribution. Entry barriers ($k_t$), which redistribute income toward the entrepreneurs who have a certain degree of monopoly power (through reducing labor demand and depressing wages), distort the allocation of resources because they prevent the entry of more productive agents into entrepreneurship. In a democracy, the most productive agents become entrepreneurs, whereas in an oligarchic society, only those who inherit firms can become entrepreneurs. Figure 1.5 shows the paths of output over time that result from the model, where $Y_t^E$ and $Y_t^D$ represent output under an oligarchy and a democracy, respectively. Initially, entrepreneurs in an oligarchic society have more productivity; however, as successive generations of less productive entrepreneurs produce the output—because those with the talent are being excluded—then entry barriers create more costs and inefficiencies. So of two otherwise identical societies, the oligarchic one will at first be richer but later will tend to fall behind the democratic society (as represented by the dashed lower curve of Figure 1.5). Whether it does so depends on whether the difference in the productivities of agents is high enough such that the cost to society of the entry barriers outweighs the cost of potentially burdensome high taxes under a democracy. The general results of the model also suggest why a democratic system may be better for long-run growth, as it allows agents with a comparative advantage in new technologies to enter entrepreneurship.

The model has many implications quite relevant for explaining the weak institutional quality in Paraguay and the low level of sustained growth. Since 1960, the small ruling oligarchy was the Colorado government, and the mostly agrarian economy generated high output with low taxation. Therefore, the distribution of resources to the rest of the population, $T_t$, was relatively small, and access to credit and education was limited mainly to the elite. Thus, Paraguay fell behind relative to its potential. A ruling political class has kept the system of

**Figure 1.5. Long-Run Output Under a Democracy and Under an Oligarchy**

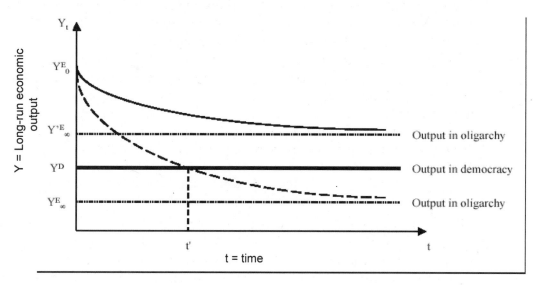

Source: Acemoglu (2003).

informality, that is, discretionary decision making, as an entry barrier (high $k_t$), which has bred corruption at all levels; there was corruption within the oligarchy because there was no incentive to break up the informal system that benefited it, and there was corruption within the rest of the population because wages were low enough and entry barriers for business high enough that the only way to increase income was to partake in the informality.

The model also predicts some stylized facts of the Paraguayan economy. It predicts the low tax rates and low hiding costs, making it easier to evade taxes. It predicts the unequal income distribution and a politically powerful, mostly agrarian productive class that is not very technologically innovative. Finally, it shows how output has fallen not only relative to its potential, but also in absolute terms since 1982, reflecting declining efficiency (negative total factor productivity). Naturally, certain aspects of Paraguay's initial conditions could be considered exogenous factors (such as the form of colonization, its natural resource endowment, and the fact that it is landlocked). However, other endogenous aspects contributed to the cycle of weak institutions and thus corruption, such as the high level of informality and the slow rate of implementation of structural reforms.

To the extent that there is greater transparency and a strengthening of democratic institutions in Paraguay, it will be easier to implement policies that broaden the tax base and reduce the costs of investment for those outside the traditional economic elite. This will lead to increased pressure to improve the institutions that favor a more productive base. Institutions will not change overnight, and, as mentioned earlier, institutions that breed corruption tend to persist. However, improved policies can set the stage for change in the right direction. One way of thinking of policies and their relationship to institutions is to consider the policies as the flow of the stock variable of institutional quality,[40] so that institutions are the cumulative outcome of past policy actions. Let $p^i_t$ denote policy dimension $i$ (where $i$ = fiscal, trade, monetary, and so forth), $I_t$ denote institutional quality at time $t$, and $\mu$ the rate at which institutional quality decays absent countervailing action, which is larger the greater is corruption. Then the evolution of institutional quality over time can be written as:

$$I_{t+1} = I_t + \eta^t_i p_i - \mu I_t,$$

where $\eta^t_i$ denotes the impact of policy $i$ on institutional quality. To the extent that higher institutional quality comes with higher income, then better policies will positively affect economic growth. At some point the second term of the equation overtakes the third and institutional quality improves. There is some empirical evidence of this. Loayza, Fajnzylber, and Calderón (2002) decompose growth in Paraguay in the 1990s into four determinants: initial conditions, structural policies, stabilization (or lack thereof), and external conditions. They find that structural reforms, in particular education reforms, were the only determinant to contribute positively to growth while also building on the stock of institutions.

## Recent initiatives

The current government has made some important steps toward breaking the vicious cycle of corruption so as to catalyze positive institutional change. Leaders of the main public sector areas have been replaced by competent and honest technocrats, renowned for their administrative abilities and not their affiliation to the ruling Colorado Party. This is the first important change. Moreover, the economic program is based on better transparency and efficiency of the public sector, which benefits investment (i.e., helps lower the entry barriers, $k$). At the same time, a sweeping fiscal reform and initial reforms in the banking sector will allow the channeling of resources to sectors of the economy that could be more productive (increasing the number of productive agents that could have firms, and increasing the level of $T_j$). The diffusion of the traditional Colorado Party power base has been more evident with the greater debate during congressional discussions over 2004 fiscal legislation aimed at broadening the tax base and raising tax revenues, although entrenched interests of the economically powerful elite exerted pressure to oppose sections that did not benefit them.

---

[40]See Rodrick, Subramanian, and Trebbi (2002).

## F. Conclusions

Corruption in Paraguay is the manifestation of the weak institutionalism that resulted from a long historical politico-economic process and has prevented Paraguay from developing productive activities, which engender sustainable long-term growth. This chapter illustrates how corruption has been an endemic aspect of the political economy of Paraguay for a long time. The direct causality is not from corruption to growth, as corruption is not a significant variable in econometric estimates once we control for other standard growth determinants. Instead, low growth and corruption are jointly determined by various outcomes that resulted from the weak institutionalism, which in turn came from its economic history. Weak institutions may breed a vicious cycle of corruption that is difficult to break, and can reduce growth by inhibiting the productive elements of a society from investing.

Paraguay is starting from a low stock of institutional quality, so it will take longer to reach a critical level that is consistent with sustainable growth. Policies that increase openness and international accountability may also be particularly effective catalysts. It will be a challenge to put in place good policies and improve governance for a long enough time to allow sustained growth to be firmly established. With enough time, however, new factions of society outside of the traditional oligarchy may begin to demand better education and a better redistribution of resources, and join the productive class.

## References

Acemoglu, Daron, 2003, "The Form of Property Rights: Oligarchic vs. Democratic Societies" (unpublished; Cambridge, Massachusetts: Massachusetts Institute of Technology, Department of Economics).

————, Simon Johnson and James A Robinson, , 2001, "The Colonial Origins of Comparative Development, An Empirical Investigation," *American Economic Review*, Vol. 91 (December), pp. 1369–1401.

————, and Yunyong Thaicharoen, 2003, "Institutional Causes, Macroeconomic Symptoms: Volatility, Crises and Growth," *Journal of Monetary Economics*, Vol. 50 (January), pp. 49–123.

Arfield, George, 2002, "Can Paraguay Move Forward from Its Corrupt Past?" *Info-America Tendencias Latin America Market Report*, No. 36 (November).

Barro, Robert, 1999, *Determinants of Economic Growth: A Cross-Country Empirical Study* (Cambridge, Massachusetts: MIT Press).

Baruja, Victor, Jorge Perez Paiva, and Ruy Pinto Schaffroth, 2003, "Una Historia de Paraguay." Available via the Internet: www.terere.com/terere/temas/paraguay/historiapy.

Centro de Información y Recursos para el Desarrollo, 2002, "Cultura Política y Prácticas de Gobernabilidad Democrática: La Ciudadanía en Su Encrucijada", Project supported by the United States Agency for International Development, Asunción.

Doppelhoffer, Gernot, Ronald Miller, and Xavier Sala-i-Martin, 2000, "Determinants of Long-Term Growth: A Bayesian Averaging of Classical Estimates (BACE) Approach," NBER Working Paper No. 7750 (Cambridge, Massachusetts: National Bureau of Economic Research).

Economist Intelligence Unit, 2003, "Country Risk Service: Risk Ratings Review" (London).

Engermann, Stanley L., and Kenneth L. Sokoloff, 1994, "Factor Endowments, Institutions and Different Paths of Growth Among New World Economies: A View from Economic Historians in the United States," NBER Working Paper No. H0066 (Cambridge, Massachusetts: National Bureau of Economic Research).

Hall, Robert, and Charles Jones, 1996, "Why Do Some Countries Produce So Much More Output per Worker Than Others?" *Quarterly Journal of Economics*, Vol. 114 (February), pp. 83–116.

———, 1999, "Levels of Economic Activity Across Countries," *American Economic Review Papers and Proceedings*, Vol. 87, pp. 173–77.

Heritage Foundation, 2003, *Index of Economic Freedom* (Washington). Available via the Internet: www.heritage.org/research/features/index/.

International Monetary Fund, 1999, *Paraguay: Estrategia de la Reforma del Sistema Tributario*, Technical Assistance Report, Fiscal Affairs Department (Washington).

———, 2000, "The Informal Sector in Paraguay," in *Paraguay: Selected Issues and Statistical Appendix*, IMF Staff Country Report No. 00/51 (Washington).

———, 2003, *Report on Observance of Standards and Codes (ROSC), Fiscal Transparency Module* (Washington).

———, and Pablo Zoido-Lobatón, 2002, "Governance Matters II—Updated Indicators for 2000/01," World Bank Policy Research Department Working Paper No. 2772 (Washington: World Bank).

Kaufmann, Daniel, Aart Kraay, and Mauro Mastruzzi, 2003, "Governance Matters III: Governance Indicators for 1996–2002," World Bank Policy Research Working Paper No. 3106 (Washington: World Bank). Available via the Internet: http://www.worldbank.org/wbi/governance/pubs/govmatters3.html.

Krueger, Anne O., 1974, "The Political Economy of the Rent-Seeking Society," *American Economic Review*, Vol. 64, No. 3, pp. 291–303.

Levine, Ross, and David Renelt, 1992, "A Sensitivity Analysis of Cross-Country Growth Regressions," *American Economic Review*, Vol. 82, No. 4, pp. 942–63.

Loayza, Norman, Pablo Fajnzylber, and Cesar Calderón, 2002, "Economic Growth in Latin America and the Caribbean, Stylized Facts, Explanations and Forecasts," World Bank Latin America Studies Paper (Washington: World Bank).

Mauro, Pablo, 2004, "The Persistence of Corruption and Slow Economic Growth," *IMF Staff Papers,* International Monetary Fund, Vol. 51, No. 1, pp. 1–18.

Murphy, Kevin M., Andrei Schleifer, and Robert Vishny, 1993, "Why Is Rent Seeking So Costly to Growth?" *American Economic Review Papers and Proceedings,* Vol. 83, No. 2, pp. 409–14.

North, Douglass C., 1981, *Structure and Change in Economic History* (New York: W.W. Norton & Co.).

Prats, J., 2002, "Diagnóstico Institucional de la República de Paraguay," United Nations Development Project (Asunción: UNDP/IIG).

Rodrick, Dani, Arvind Subramanian, and Francisco Trebbi, 2002, "Institutions Rule: The Primacy of Institutions over Geography and Integration in Economic Development" (unpublished; Cambridge, Massachusetts: Harvard University, John F. Kennedy School of Government).

Sachs, Jeffrey, and Andrew Warner, 1995, "Natural Resources, Abundance, and Economic Growth," Development Discussion Paper No. 517a (Cambridge, Massachusetts: Harvard Institute for International Development).

Sah, Raaj K., 1988, "Persistence and Pervasiveness of Corruption: New Perspectives," Yale Economic Growth Discussion Paper No. 560 (New Haven, Connecticut: Yale University).

Sala-i-Martin, Xavier, 1997, "I Just Ran Two Million Regressions," *American Economic Review*, Vol. 87, No. 2, pp. 178–83.

Schleifer, Andrei, and Robert Vishny, 1993, "Corruption," *Quarterly Journal of Economics*, Vol. 108, No. 3, pp. 599–617.

Sciscioli, Alejandro, 2003, "Nicanor Duarte Frutos to Fight Official Corruption," *Global Information Network*, July 21.

Smith, Tony, 2003, "Contraband Is Big Business in Paraguay," *New York Times*, July 10.

Tanzi, Vito, and Hamid Davoodi, 1997, "Corruption, Public Investment, and Growth," IMF Working Paper 97/139 (Washington: International Monetary Fund).

Tobar, Hector, 2002, "About as Corrupt as It Gets," *Los Angeles Times*, December 14.

Transparency International, 2003, "2003 Corruption Perception Index,", Available via the Internet: http://www.transparency.org/cpi/2003/cpi2003.en.html.

United States, Department of Commerce, 1999, *Paraguay Investment Climate Report*, National Trade Data Bank, September 1999, Washington.

World Bank, 1996, "Paraguay: The Role of the State," World Bank Country Report No. 15044-PA (Washington: World Bank).

———, 2003a, "Country Assistance Strategy of the World Bank for the Republic of Paraguay," World Bank Report No. 27341-PA (Washington: World Bank).

———, 2003b, "Improving Governance and Accountability in Public Institutions," in *Paraguay Policy Options for the New Administration: Creating Conditions for Sustainable Growth*, World Bank Report No. 25894-PA (Washington: World Bank).

# 1

# A Political Economy Model of Output Growth

The following reduced-form model, developed in detail in Acemoglu (2003), presents the tradeoff between an oligarchic and a democratic society. Under each society, agents vote for the level of taxes at every period $t$ ($\tau_t$), which redistribute income from entrepreneurs to workers, as well as the level of entry barriers ($k$), which redistribute income toward the entrepreneurs who will have a certain degree of monopoly power as a result, thus preventing the entry of more productive agents into entrepreneurship.

Each agent $j$ can either be employed as a worker or set up a firm to become an entrepreneur. While all agents have the same productivity as workers, their productivity in entrepreneurship differs. To become an entrepreneur, an agent needs to set up a firm, or, alternatively, he could inherit the firm from a parent. The agent chooses the occupational choice $i = 0$ (a worker) or $i = 1$ (an entrepreneur). Setting up a new firm will be costly because of the entry barriers created by existing entrepreneurs. Each agent therefore starts period t with a level of bequest (income) $b^j_t$; entrepreneurial talent $a^j_t \in \{A^H, A^L\}$, where $A^H > A^L$; and $s^j_t$, which denotes whether he either inherits or does not inherit a firm (where $s^j_t \in \{0,1\}$). By definition, if agent $j$ at time $t$ sets up a firm, then his offspring inherits the firm, so $s_{t+1} = i^j_t$. All agents in the economy work in the firm and receive wages, but only some become entrepreneurs. They must choose the amount of investment effort ($e^j_t$), employment ($l^j_t$), and tax evasion technology ($b^j_t$) to maximize profit, given the other parameters.

Society as a whole every period chooses a tax rate $\tau_t$ (a tax on output), which determines aggregate $T_t$ (the level of lump-sum transfers to all agents) and $K_t > 0$ (the fixed cost to set up a new firm). If the cost of hiding/evading taxes is $\delta$, then taxes will be non-zero as long as $0 < \delta < \tau_t$. If $s^j_t = 0$ for an agent $j$ (he has not inherited a firm), then in the presence of entry barriers he must incur a cost $k_t = K_t/\lambda$ to run a firm (where $\lambda$ is the maximum capacity per firm). The net gain from becoming an entrepreneur for an agent of type ($s_t$, $a_t$) as a function of the policy vector $\{\tau_t, k_t\}$ and wage rate $w_t$ is:

$$\Pi(k_t, \tau_t, w_t / s^j_t, a^j_t) = \underset{l^j_t, e^j_t}{Max}(\tau_t, l^j_t, e^j_t, a^j_t, w_t) - (1 - s^j_t)k_t\lambda.$$

Acemoglu specifies a Markov process to determine the talent distribution across time, hence the productivity of agents across generations. The productivity of an agent $j$ at time $t + 1$ can be either high or low ($A^H$ or $A^L$) according to the following probabilities:

$$
a_{t+1}^j = \begin{cases} A^H \text{ with probability } \sigma_H & \text{if } a_t^j = A^H, \\ A^H \text{ with probability } \sigma_L & \text{if } a_t^j = A^L, \\ A^L \text{ with probability } 1 - \sigma_H & \text{if } a_t^j = A^H, \\ A^L \text{ with probability } 1 - \sigma_L & \text{if } a_t^j = A^L. \end{cases}
$$

where $\sigma^H$ is the probability that an agent has high productivity conditional on his parent being productive. It is also assumed that workers are the majority of the population and that investment decisions are made before taxation decisions. Then, under reasonable parameters and a stationary Markov process, it turns out that agents with $a_t^j = A^L$ and $s_t^j = 0$ (unproductive agents without an inheritance) will always find it optimal to become workers and vote for a high tax. Conversely, if $a_t^j = A^H$ and $s_t^j = 1$, the productive agent is always better off being an entrepreneur.

Aggregating, two different types of equilibrium are defined and shown to exist. First, an "entry" equilibrium, in which only productive agents become entrepreneurs (they have $a_t^j = A^H$). This equilibrium holds if the following condition is true:

$$
\frac{\alpha}{(1-\alpha)}(1-\tau)^{1/\alpha}(A^H - A^L) \geq K_t,
$$

where $\alpha$ is the (Cobb-Douglas) production function coefficient. Second, if the inverse holds true, we obtain a "sclerotic" equilibrium, defined as an equilibrium where only those who inherit firms ($s_t^j = 1$) become entrepreneurs, regardless of their productivity. The equilibrium wage rate $w_t$ and levels of labor $l_t$ can therefore be determined based on labor demand by entrepreneurs under each type of equilibrium, given an inelastic labor supply (since entrepreneurs also work).

In a politico-economic context, a *democracy* is defined within the model as a society where the entry barriers and tax levels $k_t$ and $\tau_t$, respectively, are determined by majoritarian voting (one agent, one vote), and an *oligarchy* is defined as a society where the outcome $k_t$ and $\tau_t$ are determined by majority voting by the elite only, where an agent is a member of the elite at time $t$ if he inherited a firm ($s_t^j = 1$).

Under a democracy, it turns out that taxes are chosen to maximize per capita transfers, in large part because workers are in the majority and can maximize their income ex post, given wages, by having higher taxes. They will choose a tax rate $\tau_t = \delta$, the maximum level possible given the tax evasion technology, and eliminate entry barriers ($k_t = 0$). Under an oligarchic society, the only heterogeneity within the elite is between high- and low-productivity agents. Acemoglu (2003) shows that under reasonable parameters, both low- and high-productivity elites will have the same preferences and will vote for high entry barriers ($k_t = k^E$) and low taxes ($\tau_t = 0$). This results in the equilibrium wage rate $w^E_t = 0$. One feature of the equilibrium under an oligarchy, therefore, is that there is a high degree of earnings inequality.

The following equations compare output over time under a democracy ($Y^D_t$) and under an oligarchy ($Y^E_t$). It turns out that output under a democracy in the model is constant, whereas output under an oligarchy depends on the productivity states over time:

$$Y^D = \frac{1}{(1-\alpha)}(1-\delta)^{\frac{(1-\alpha)}{\alpha}} A^H < Y^E_0 = \frac{1}{(1-\alpha)} A^H.$$

Aggregate output in the first period under an oligarchy ($Y^E_0$) is always greater than under democracy. However, $Y^E_t$ declines over time, while $Y^D$ is constant. Consequently, the oligarchic economy subsequently falls behind the democratic society. Whether it does so ($Y^E_\infty < Y^D$) depends on the following condition:

$$(1-\delta)^{\frac{1-\alpha}{\alpha}} \quad > \quad \frac{A^L}{A^H} + \left(\frac{\sigma_L}{(1-\sigma_H - \sigma_L)}\right)\left(1 - \frac{A^L}{A^H}\right).$$

In other words, democracy's output eventually overtakes an oligarchy's output if the taxes $\delta$ set under a democracy are not too high to stifle investment ($Y_D$ is not too low), and the difference in the productivity of agents ($1 - A^L/A^H$) is high enough that forgoing having productive agents to run firms is not too costly to society. This is illustrated by the upper curve in Figure 1.5.

# 2 Financial Crises and Behavior of Private Sector Credit in Paraguay

## A. Introduction

A series of financial crises have afflicted Paraguay since the financial liberalization in the 1990s and have contributed to the fall in private sector credit. Paraguay did not reap all the benefits associated with financial liberalization because of a lack of adequate banking regulation and supervision; inadequate banking skills, including poor credit and risk assessment; and bad banking practices, such as high levels of insider lending and excessive loan concentration. These weaknesses culminated in the demise of 13 banks and 35 financial companies between 1995 and 1998. In 2002, given the strong link with the Argentine economy, Paraguayans began to hastily withdraw their deposits, bringing about the closure of Banco Alemán and four finance companies. In 2003, the closure of a locally owned private bank and four finance companies, as well as the voluntary withdrawal of three banks, further led to a loss of confidence in the financial system.

This chapter examines the current state of the financial system, the financial crises since the mid-1990s, and the behavior of private sector credit in Paraguay in 2003. First, it assesses the current state of the financial sector, drawing from a comprehensive financial sector survey. It is the only detailed financial sector survey on Paraguay in the literature. Second, the study presents an overview of the financial crises since the 1990s. Third, it analyzes private sector credit in 2003 using detailed data on banks and finance companies. Finally, it draws conclusions and makes policy recommendations.

The waves of financial crises, in a context of political and macroeconomic instability, affected both credit supply and demand, hampering growth prospects. Poor public finances, including the government default on treasury bonds held by banks, affected the liquidity of the latter. In addition, the fall in credit supply can be attributed to the lack of a more flexible liquidity support facility, lack of long-term financing sources, high levels of nonperforming loans (NPLs), lack of hedging instruments against exchange rate volatility, and the relative increase of the informal economy. In parallel, the demand for credit fell because of the recession, the high cost of intermediation, and the unfavorable investment climate, including weak legal institutions and rule of law.

The recurring financial crises in Paraguay point to the need for financial sector reforms. The authorities started implementing the recently approved financial resolution law and new financial regulations. The financial resolution law expedites the resolution process by establishing clear procedures for bank intervention and resolution, and by introducing a deposit insurance fund. The new financial regulations include more stringent rules on asset classification, recognition of credit risk, provision requirements, and imputation of accrued interest. The authorities should press ahead with the approval of the Public Banking Law to consolidate public-lending institutions, and with a comprehensive banking law. Moreover, they should remain vigilant to developments in the financial sector by closely monitoring financial indicators, which serve as early warning signals against potential risks, and by taking prompt corrective action when needed.

## B. Current State of the Financial System

The financial system consists of deposit institutions, nondeposit institutions, and other financial institutions.[41] The deposit institutions include banks, finance companies, savings and loans associations, cooperatives, an investment fund, and a mutual fund. The nondeposit institutions comprise insurance companies, pensions systems, public financial entities, and warehouses.[42] The other financial institutions include the stock market and money exchange houses.

### Banking system

The banking system dominates the financial sector, with about 72 percent of assets (Figure 2.1). It consists of six wholly foreign-owned banks, five majority-owned foreign banks, two locally owned private banks, and a public development bank, Banco Nacional del Fomento (BNF). Wholly foreign-owned banks control the market, followed by the majority-owned foreign banks, and locally owned banks.

---

[41]For a more comprehensive analysis of the financial system in Paraguay see Appendix 1 in this chapter, which contains questions based on a survey by Creane et al. (2004). The survey collects data on a wide range of financial system issues including questions that represent different facets of financial development, such as development of the monetary system and monetary policy, banking system, other financial entities, financial regulation and supervision, financial openness and exchange rate, and institutional and legal environment.

[42]Warehouses and the savings and loans associations account for only 1 percent of financial assets.

## Figure 2.1 . Financial Institution's Market Share

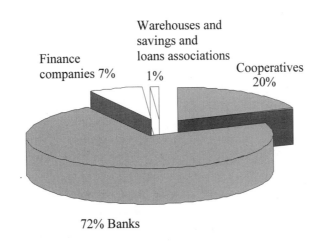

Sources: INCOOP; Superintendency of Banks; and IMF staff estimates.

The BNF was created in 1961 to promote various economic sectors. The BNF is the seventh largest bank, with 8 percent of banking assets. The BNF has the largest branch network, with 49 branches covering rural areas, and both retail and wholesale operations. It employs 946 employees, corresponding to 35 percent of the total in the banking system. The bank is the first-largest lender to the agricultural sector, with a market share of about 19 percent, and the second-largest to the manufacturing sector, with a market share of 14 percent. Besides the BNF, there are seven public entities that channel subsidized funds, mainly from the international donor community. Five (CAH, FG, FDC, BANAVI, CONAVI) of these seven entities are first-tier institutions, whereas the other two (UTEP, FDI) are second-tier institutions.

Although overall bank credit supply declined by 17 percent in 2003, credit in some banks increased (Tables 2.1 and 2.2).[43, 44] Wholly foreign-owned banks reduced credit supply by 29 percent. Only three (Citibank, Lloyds, and ABN) of the six wholly foreign-owned banks held 43 percent of total assets. Citibank

---

[43]Insfran (1999) found a correlation between lower credit supply and a high concentration of deposits in Paraguay, in a sample of 28 banks for 1996–98.

[44]Data for the first five months of 2004 seem to suggest a rebound in bank credit supply. However, it is early to infer that a reversal of trend is under way, as bank credit continued to decline in the year leading up to May 2004.

### Table 2.1. Size, Credit, and Deposits of Financial Institutions, 2002–03

| | | | 2002 | | |
|---|---|---|---|---|---|
| | | | Assets/ Total | Credit | Deposits |
| | Branches | Personnel | (In percent) | (In billions of guaraníes) | |
| Total financial system | 248 | 4,837 | 100 | 7,570 | 10,060 |
| Banks | 164 | 3,188 | 100 | 6,790 | 9,302 |
| *Wholly foreign-owned banks* | 27 | 839 | 48 | 2,838 | 4,748 |
| Citibank N.A. | 7 | 200 | 17 | 884 | 1,695 |
| Lloyds TSB Bank P.L.C. | 6 | 188 | 10 | 655 | 940 |
| ABN Amro Bank N.V. | 8 | 246 | 15 | 837 | 1,493 |
| Banco do Brasil S.A. | 1 | 62 | 3 | 201 | 285 |
| Banco de la Nación Argentina | 3 | 74 | 1 | 79 | 80 |
| I.N.G. Barings N.V. | 0 | 28 | 2 | 108 | 187 |
| Chinatrust Commercial Bank | 2 | 41 | 1 | 75 | 68 |
| *Majority-owned foreign banks* | 45 | 849 | 33 | 2,284 | 3,110 |
| Banco Asunción S.A. | 1 | 61 | 1 | 62 | 95 |
| Interbanco S.A. | 10 | 173 | 8 | 559 | 788 |
| Banco Sudameris S.A.E.C.A. | 10 | 188 | 10 | 773 | 879 |
| Banco Bilbao Viscaya Argentaria Paraguay S.A. | 7 | 97 | 9 | 547 | 860 |
| Banco del Paraná S.A. | 0 | 70 | 1 | 42 | 46 |
| Banco Integración S.A. | 4 | 83 | 2 | 153 | 215 |
| Banco Continental S.A.E.C.A. | 13 | 177 | 2 | 147 | 228 |
| *Locally owned private banks* | 43 | 572 | 10 | 918 | 906 |
| Banco Regional S.A. | 11 | 134 | 3 | 220 | 276 |
| Banco Amambay S.A. | 4 | 92 | 2 | 124 | 195 |
| Multibanco S.A.E.C.A. | 28 | 346 | 5 | 575 | 435 |
| *Public development bank* | 49 | 928 | 8 | 749 | 538 |
| Banco Nacional de Fomento | 49 | 928 | 8 | 749 | 538 |
| Finance companies | 84 | 1,649 | | 780 | 758 |

reduced its operations significantly, maintaining only its corporate banking. While its deposits declined by 12 percent, credit fell by 36 percent. ABN reduced credit by 16 percent, and Lloyds by 24 percent. On the contrary, majority-owned foreign banks, with 37 percent of total assets, increased credit by 11 percent. All banks in this group, except for Continental, which has recently merged with a finance company, increased credit supply. Regional, a locally owned private bank expanded by 42 percent, recording the highest growth.

## Table 2.1 *(concluded)*

| | Branches | Personnel | 2003 Assets/ Total (In percent) | Credit (In billions of | Deposits guaraníes) | Percentage Change (2002–03) Credit | Deposits |
|---|---|---|---|---|---|---|---|
| **Total financial system** | 233 | 4,606 | 100 | 6,544 | 10,947 | −13.5 | 8.8 |
| **Banks** | 127 | 2,680 | 100 | 5,648 | 9,886 | −16.8 | 6.3 |
| *Wholly foreign-owned banks* | 22 | 803 | 47 | 2,029 | 4,748 | −28.5 | 0.0 |
| Citibank N.A. | 6 | 179 | 15 | 563 | 1,491 | −36.4 | −12.1 |
| Lloyds TSB Bank P.L.C. | 6 | 221 | 12 | 498 | 1,194 | −24.0 | 27.0 |
| ABN Amro Bank N.V. | 6 | 236 | 16 | 705 | 1,638 | −15.8 | 9.7 |
| Banco do Brasil S.A. | 1 | 61 | 3 | 150 | 266 | −25.0 | −6.8 |
| Banco de la Nación Argentina | 3 | 74 | 1 | 70 | 114 | −10.7 | 43.2 |
| I.N.G. Barings N.V. | . . . | . . . | . . . | . . . | . . . | . . . | . . . |
| Chinatrust Commercial Bank | 0 | 32 | 1 | 43 | 46 | −42.7 | −32.7 |
| *Majority-owned foreign banks* | 41 | 681 | 37 | 2,527 | 3,769 | 10.7 | 21.2 |
| Banco Asunción S.A. | | | | | | | |
| Interbanco S.A. | 10 | 173 | 12 | 614 | 1,238 | 9.9 | 57.1 |
| Banco Sudameris S.A.E.C.A. | 9 | 184 | 9 | 1,023 | 869 | 32.2 | −1.1 |
| Banco Bilbao Viscaya Argentaria Paraguay S.A. | 7 | 97 | 11 | 598 | 1,162 | 9.3 | 35.2 |
| Banco del Paraná S.A. | | | | | | | |
| Banco Integración S.A. | 6 | 89 | 3 | 180 | 283 | 17.9 | 32.0 |
| Banco Continental S.A.E.C.A. | 9 | 138 | 2 | 112 | 216 | −23.9 | −5.0 |
| *Locally owned private banks* | 15 | 250 | 7 | 436 | 716 | −52.5 | −21.0 |
| | 11 | 154 | 5 | 312 | 449 | 41.8 | 62.8 |
| Multibanco S.A.E.C.A. | 4 | 96 | 3 | 125 | 267 | 0.8 | 37.1 |
| *Public development bank* | 49 | 946 | 8 | 655 | 654 | −12.5 | 21.4 |
| Banco Nacional de Fomento | 49 | 946 | 8 | 655 | 654 | −12.5 | 21.4 |
| **Finance companies** | 106 | 1,926 | . . . | 897 | 1,061 | 14.9 | 40.0 |

Source: Superintendency of Banks.

Wholly foreign-owned banks financed mainly wholesale commerce—a stagnant sector in Paraguay now—while majority-owned foreign banks and locally owned private banks financed the booming agricultural sector. Credit to the agricultural sector represented 22 percent of the total, and to the wholesale commerce, 20 percent in 2003. Over the past years, favorable production and prices of soy contributed to the dynamism of banks financing the agricultural sector. In contrast, banks financing other sectors of the economy have stagnated as a result of the economic recession.

## Table 2.2. Macroeconomic and Financial Indicators, 1995–2003
*(In percent, unless otherwise specified)*

|  | 1995 | 1996 | 1997 | 1998 | 1999 | 2000 | 2001 | 2002 | 2003 |
|---|---|---|---|---|---|---|---|---|---|
| **Commercial banks** | | | | | | | | | |
| *Market structure* | | | | | | | | | |
| *Number of banks* (units) | 35 | 32 | 33 | 23 | 22 | 22 | 20 | 18 | 14 |
| Wholly foreign-owned | 13 | 14 | 9 | 9 | 9 | 9 | 8 | 7 | 6 |
| Majority-owned foreign | ... | ... | 9 | 8 | 7 | 8 | 8 | 7 | 5 |
| Locally owned private banks | 20 | 16 | 13 | 5 | 5 | 4 | 3 | 3 | 2 |
| Public development bank | 2 | 2 | 2 | 1 | 1 | 1 | 1 | 1 | 1 |
| *Share in assets* | | | | | | | | | |
| Wholly foreign-owned | 45.9 | 43.8 | 34.9 | 46.6 | 48.3 | 47.0 | 45.1 | 48.4 | 47.4 |
| Majority-owned foreign | ... | ... | 26.7 | 32.2 | 29.9 | 34.9 | 38.3 | 33.2 | 37.2 |
| Locally owned private banks | 35.8 | 37.8 | 19.7 | 8.2 | 9.1 | 6.8 | 7.4 | 10.4 | 7.4 |
| Public development bank | 18.3 | 18.4 | 18.7 | 13.0 | 12.7 | 11.4 | 9.2 | 8.0 | 8.0 |
| *Capital* | | | | | | | | | |
| Capital-adequacy ratio (percent) | 19.5 | 18.2 | 21.2 | 20.7 | 17.4 | 17.6 | 16.9 | 17.9 | 20.9 |
| *Asset quality* | | | | | | | | | |
| NPLs (percent) total loans | 7.9 | 11.1 | 13.1 | 11.8 | 14.8 | 16.6 | 16.5 | 19.7 | 20.6 |
| Provisions (percent) NPLs | ... | 41.6 | 41.0 | 34.9 | 40.1 | 38.8 | 37.0 | 46.6 | 54.8 |
| *Profitability* | | | | | | | | | |
| Rate of return on assets (ROA) | 1.9 | 2.4 | 2.8 | 3.4 | 2.2 | 1.4 | 2.2 | 1.0 | 0.4 |
| Rate of return on equity (ROE) | 13.5 | 21.0 | 23.2 | 28.0 | 20.1 | 12.4 | 21.2 | 9.0 | 4.5 |
| *Deposit structure* | | | | | | | | | |
| Current account and sight deposits in total | 73.0 | 71.9 | 66.2 | 68.8 | 66.7 | 64.5 | 65.2 | 67.3 | 76.9 |
| Term deposits, CDs, and investment titles in total | 27.0 | 28.1 | 33.8 | 31.2 | 33.3 | 35.5 | 34.8 | 32.7 | 23.1 |
| *Interest rates* | | | | | | | | | |
| Weighted average lending rate in local currency | 33.3 | 30.6 | 27.1 | 32.0 | 28.7 | 26.4 | 31.4 | 53.6 | 36.2 |
| Weighted average lending rate in foreign exchange currency | 14.0 | 14.9 | 12.6 | 12.1 | 12.3 | 11.5 | 9.3 | 9.5 | 8.2 |
| *Holdings at the BCP* (billions of PARG) | 1,204 | 1,402 | 1,457 | 1,618 | 1,689 | 1,772 | 2,263 | 2,545 | 3,684 |
| Deposits in the BCP | 1,032 | 1,172 | 1,187 | 1,418 | 1,631 | 1,734 | 2,100 | 2,247 | 3,083 |
| Holdings of LRM | 172 | 230 | 270 | 200 | 58 | 38 | 163 | 298 | 602 |
| **Finance companies** | | | | | | | | | |
| *Market structure* | | | | | | | | | |
| Number of finance companies (units) | 68.0 | 54.0 | 50.0 | 36.0 | 33.0 | 28.0 | 25.0 | 21.0 | 17.0 |
| *Capital* | | | | | | | | | |
| Capital adequacy ratio | 29.0 | 27.6 | 24.1 | 21.2 | 27.5 | 25.1 | 21.0 | 19.2 | 18.6 |
| *Asset quality* | | | | | | | | | |
| Nonperforming loan | 13.9 | 16.2 | 9.2 | 9.6 | 14.9 | 11.0 | 10.7 | 15.1 | 10.4 |
| Provisions (percent) nonperforming loans | ... | 52.2 | 41.9 | 45.1 | 47.1 | 45.7 | 49.1 | 45.1 | 45.8 |
| *Profitability* | | | | | | | | | |
| Returns on assets | 1.2 | 1.9 | 6.2 | 6.1 | 3.6 | 4.4 | 5.1 | 2.3 | 1.6 |
| Returns on equity | 4.6 | 14.6 | 27.1 | 24.6 | 12.6 | 18.5 | 24.2 | 10.7 | 8.3 |

## Table 2.2 *(concluded)*

| | 1995 | 1996 | 1997 | 1998 | 1999 | 2000 | 2001 | 2002 | 2003 |
|---|---|---|---|---|---|---|---|---|---|
| *Deposit structure* | | | | | | | | | |
| Sight deposits in total | 0.0 | 1.2 | 2.3 | 4.5 | 6.7 | 8.4 | 10.4 | 13.6 | 18.3 |
| Term deposits, CDs, and investment titles in total | 100.0 | 98.8 | 97.7 | 95.5 | 93.3 | 91.6 | 89.6 | 86.4 | 81.7 |
| *Interest rates* | | | | | | | | | |
| Weighted average lending rate in local currency | . . . | . . . | 47.0 | 51.2 | 52.4 | 50.4 | 52.7 | 55.1 | 43.5 |
| Weighted average lending rate in foreign exchange currency | . . . | . . . | 18.1 | 18.5 | 18.7 | 15.5 | 15.6 | 15.9 | 14.5 |
| *Holdings at the BCP* (billions of PARG) | 48.3 | 53.0 | 69.0 | 76.9 | 77.9 | 98.2 | 107.4 | 106.7 | 117.5 |
| Deposits in the BCP | 47.0 | 52.6 | 69.0 | 73.7 | 72.8 | 92.2 | 105.3 | 100.7 | 117.5 |
| Holdings of LRM | 1.3 | 0.4 | 0.0 | 3.2 | 5.0 | 6.0 | 2.1 | 5.9 | 0.0 |
| State of the economy | | | | | | | | | |
| Real GDP growth | 4.7 | 1.3 | 2.6 | −0.4 | 0.5 | −0.4 | 2.7 | −2.3 | 2.3 |
| Growth in real investment | 7.1 | −0.1 | −2.0 | −4.7 | -3.8 | −0.7 | −17.5 | −11.0 | −3.6 |
| Inflation | 10.5 | 8.2 | 6.2 | 14.6 | 5.4 | 8.6 | 8.4 | 14.6 | 9.3 |
| Exchange rate depreciation (−) (US$ per PARG) | −3.1 | −5.9 | −9.5 | −18 | −14.3 | −6.5 | −23.5 | −33.8 | 15.3 |
| Central government balance as percent of GDP | −0.3 | −1.1 | −1.4 | −1.0 | −3.6 | −2.9 | −4.4 | −2.3 | −0.3 |
| M2 growth | . . . | 0.2 | 5.5 | −2.9 | 10.7 | 2.2 | 4.9 | −2.2 | 24.9 |
| Interest rate on central bank bills | 12.7 | 9.5 | 15.5 | 26.2 | 13.2 | 5.9 | 21.0 | 24.7 | 12.9 |
| International reserves (in millions of U.S. dollars) | 1,106 | 1,062 | 846 | 875 | 988 | 772 | 723 | 641 | 982 |
| Current account as percent of GDP | −1.0 | −3.7 | −6.8 | −1.9 | −2.1 | −2.1 | −4.0 | 1.7 | 2.0 |
| Terms of trade (deterioration −) | . . . | 0.5 | −2.5 | −1.0 | 2.3 | −4.6 | −0.1 | 7.4 | 6.4 |

Sources: Paraguayan authorities; and Fund staff estimates.

Wholly foreign-owned banks performed less favorably than other banks in 2003 (Table 2.3 and Figure 2.2). The NPL ratios in wholly foreign-owned banks were higher than in the majority-owned foreign banks and locally owned private banks. The fall in credit (the denominator) worsened these ratios. The continuous deterioration in NPL ratios in wholly foreign-owned banks weakened profitability. Consequently, returns on assets (ROA) in wholly foreign-owned banks were lower than in majority-owned foreign banks and in locally owned private banks. Wholly foreign-owned banks also had higher administrative costs than majority-owned foreign banks. Among private banks, wholly foreign-owned banks had the highest share of sight deposits to total deposits (80 percent).

Banks reduced credit supply and started to build excess liquidity (33 percent of total assets). Since the fall of Banco Alemán, banks began to hold more risk-free assets, such as holdings of central bank bills and unremunerated excess deposits

### Table 2.3. Selected Financial Indicators, 2003
#### (In percent)

| | NPLs | ROA | Provisions as a Share of NPLs | Liquid Assets as a Share of Deposits | Aministrative Spending over Deposits | Sight Deposits/ Total | Term Deposits/ Total |
|---|---|---|---|---|---|---|---|
| **Total banks** | 20.6 | 0.6 | 65.0 | 52.7 | 6.1 | 76.9 | 23.1 |
| *Wholly foreign-owned banks* | 20.7 | 0.3 | 71.9 | 51.9 | 5.9 | 80.4 | 19.6 |
| Citibank N.A. | 29.3 | −1.5 | 61.1 | 44.3 | 7.3 | 70.7 | 29.3 |
| Lloyds TSB Bank P.L.C. | 15.5 | 1.1 | 56.6 | 57.9 | 4.9 | 85.4 | 14.6 |
| ABN Amro Bank N.V. | 15.1 | 1.6 | 105.9 | 49.3 | 4.7 | 86.0 | 14.0 |
| Banco do Brasil S.A. | 17.9 | 1.8 | 145.6 | 71.1 | 6.2 | 74.0 | 26.0 |
| Banco de la Nación Argentina | 24.8 | −1.0 | 61.7 | 81.0 | 9.8 | 90.8 | 9.2 |
| Chinatrust Commercial Bank | 30.4 | −6.1 | 42.2 | 57.2 | 20.3 | 74.2 | 25.8 |
| *Majority-owned foreign banks* | 12.3 | 1.4 | 80.6 | 54.2 | 4.8 | 73.1 | 26.9 |
| Interbanco S.A. | 8.0 | 1.2 | 92.9 | 59.5 | 4.4 | 79.6 | 20.4 |
| Banco Sudameris S.A.E.C.A. | 29.2 | −2.0 | 63.4 | 42.6 | 6.2 | 69.4 | 30.6 |
| Banco Bilbao Viscaya Argentaria Paraguay S.A. | 2.6 | 4.5 | 239.0 | 56.0 | 2.5 | 67.2 | 32.8 |
| Banco Integración S.A. | 3.9 | 1.3 | 77.9 | 54.2 | 6.3 | 76.8 | 23.2 |
| Banco Continental S.A.E.C.A. | 12.7 | 0.2 | 66.9 | 60.7 | 11.9 | 77.9 | 22.1 |
| *Locally-owned private banks* | 3.1 | 1.9 | 72.8 | 55.7 | 6.1 | 68.2 | 31.8 |
| Banco Regional S.A. | 1.2 | 2.5 | 135.2 | 49.2 | 5.9 | 67.3 | 32.7 |
| Banco Amambay S.A. | 8.5 | 0.7 | 48.4 | 66.8 | 6.5 | 69.7 | 30.3 |
| *Public development bank* | 56.2 | −2.8 | 47.7 | 46.2 | 14.4 | 83.6 | 16.4 |
| Banco Nacional de Fomento | 56.2 | −2.8 | 47.7 | 46.2 | 14.4 | 83.6 | 16.4 |
| **Finance companies** | **10.4** | **1.6** | **45.8** | **32.6** | **14.7** | **18.3** | **81.7** |

Source: Superientendency of Banks.

at the Central Bank of Paraguay (BCP) (Figure 2.3). Banks doubled central bank bill holdings to PARG 602 billion in December 2003 and increased excess deposits at the BCP to PARG 500 billion in 2003. Central bank bills during 2002 and 2003 offered attractive interest rates, although they have dropped significantly over the past months. In contrast, excess deposits are unremunerated but are immediately available, causing concerns for monetary policy.

Credit supplied by the BNF also contracted in 2003, partly owing to its new loan limits and high NPL ratios. The authorities imposed loan limits because of the widespread perception of corruption in this bank and of political clientelism.[45]

---

[45]Transparency International ranked Paraguay tied for ninety-eighth out of 102 countries in its corruption perception index in 2002, the worst ranking in Latin America. This poor ranking reflects in part the perceived inadequacy of public sector institutions—the country ranked seventy-fourth out of 75 in its public institutions.

**Figure 2.2. Financial Indicators, 2003**
*(In percent)*

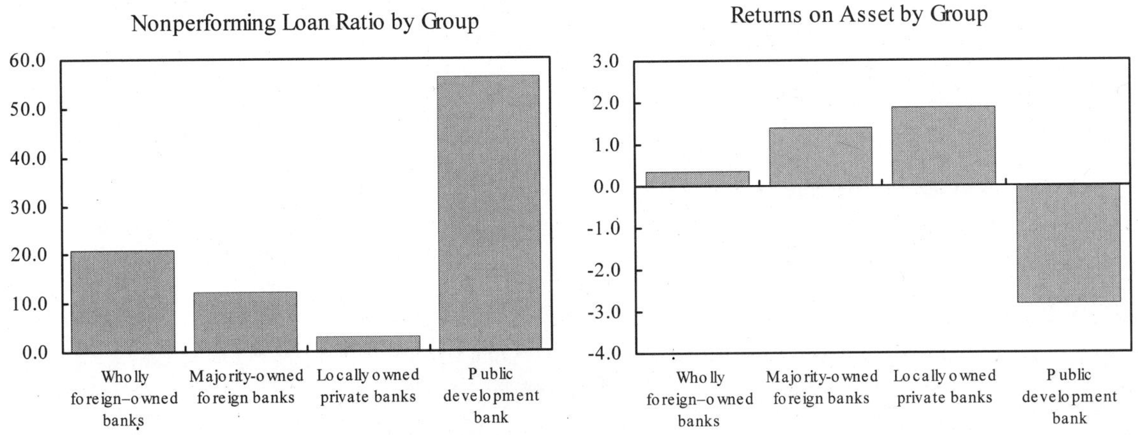

Sources: Superintendency of Banks, and Fund staff estimates.

One-year loans are limited to PARG 100 million per corporation, three-year loans to PARG 300 million, and five-year loan maturity to PARG 700 million. The NPL ratios are very high (56 percent). Systematic operating losses and poor use of resources caused most of BNF's liquidity problems. Political influence further distorted the bank's operations by affecting loan approvals and by forcing the bank to provide subsidies without the corresponding fiscal resources. BNF loans are concentrated among a few dozen well-connected clients; two-thirds of its loans are to less than 5 percent of clients. Of past-due loans, the 50 largest loans, representing half of all past-due loans in December 1999, were owed by 0.3 percent of total clients. Furthermore, the bank has been unable to prosecute large but influential delinquent borrowers successfully. In the interim, the BNF has been recapitalized and its operations are being modernized and streamlined. So far, the bank has not experienced liquidity problems.

## Finance companies

Finance companies, with about 7 percent of assets, extend mainly microcredit. There are 17 finance companies, but 2 are in liquidation, and 1 recently merged with a bank. NPL ratios were 10 percent, compared with 15 percent in private banks, and ROA was 1.6 percent in December 2003. The Superintendency of Banks (SB) regulates and supervises finance companies.

### Figure 2.3. Liquid Assets of Banks
*(In billions of guaraníes)*

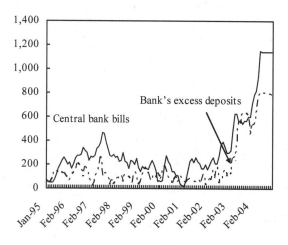

Source: Central Bank of Paraguay.

## Cooperative sector

The cooperative sector, with 20 percent of financial assets, plays an important economic and social role in Paraguay. Three types of cooperatives—financial, production, and other cooperatives—exist. Financial cooperatives provide microcredit to 90 percent of its members. The production cooperatives finance agricultural and dairy products, and other cooperatives provide goods, services, and employment. There are about 820 registered cooperatives, out of which 525 are financial cooperatives, and 200 are production cooperatives. However, preliminary data show that more than half of the cooperatives have ceased operations. The cooperative sector helps promote education by funding the Education Development Cooperative Fund, with at least 10 percent of its dividends. In 2002, cooperative sector deposits stood at US$154 million and assets at US$464 million.

The largest 25 financial cooperatives, with 356,000 members, accounted for 80 percent of financial cooperative assets (Gamarra, 2004a and b). Their deposits amounted to about US$82 million and credit to US$110 million. These institutions are highly liquid, with a capital adequacy ratio (CAR) of 34 percent. With the excess liquidity, financial cooperatives intend to finance production cooperatives.

## Figure 2.4. Selected Indicators of the Largest 25 Financial Cooperatives

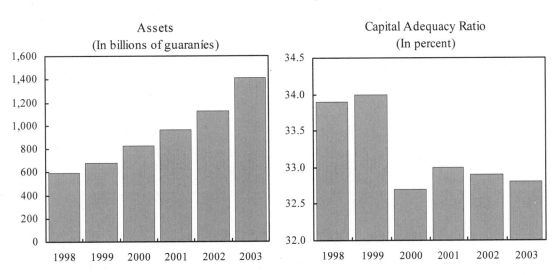

Sources: Superintendency of Banks; and Fund staff estimates.

The assets of the largest 25 financial cooperatives have more than doubled since 1998 (Figure 2.4). Because of several banking crises, the public started to shift savings from the banking system to the cooperative sector. Consequently, some cooperatives began to provide services that previously were offered only by banks, except for current accounts and foreign exchange operations. Contrary to banks, cooperatives conduct most of their operations in local currency.

The supervisory authority of the cooperatives, INCOOP, began taking steps to introduce supervision of the cooperatives by January 2005. It requested assistance from international cooperatives and institutions for (1) implementing prudential norms, (2) designing balance sheets, (3) incorporating the cooperatives into the credit rating agency, (4) providing training, (5) implementing money laundering regulations, and (6) setting a deposit insurance guarantee.

## C. Overview of the Financial Crises

### Precrises situation

During most of the 1980s, policies of financial repression dominated the financial sector in Paraguay.[46] These policies included controlled interest rates,

---

[46]See Penner (1994), Garcia-Herrero (1997a), Straub (1998), Ashwell (2000), Insfran (2000), and Shogo and Habermeier (2002) for a detailed analysis of the 1995–98 financial sector crisis in Paraguay.

high reserve requirement rates (42 percent), fixed exchange rates, and credit controls. Banks had to finance agricultural exports through rediscount papers, which were rediscounted at subsidized rates at the BCP. Moreover, public sector deposits could be located only at the BCP.

By 1989, with a change in government, Paraguay embarked on a process of financial liberalization, which continued through the mid-1990s. The authorities introduced a unified, managed floating exchange rate regime, liberalized interest rates, reduced reserve requirements, gradually eliminated the rediscount papers at the BCP, and issued norms for asset classification. From 1990 to 1993, the authorities further reduced reserve requirements and freed public sector deposits from the BCP to the banking system. In November 1994, financial transactions could be carried out also in foreign currency, allowing banks to extend loans denominated in foreign currency.

Banks started to pursue aggressive accounting practices, exacerbated by poor management.[47] Financial institutions recorded in their accounting books nonexistent assets, lent to related parties, and registered only part of their liabilities. Some financial institutions kept unrecorded deposits off balance sheet in a second accounting book system. Unrecorded deposits could be "grey" or "black." Grey deposits, for which adequate documentation existed, had been recorded off balance sheet, and black deposits, such as promissory notes, were based on inadequate documentation. Most Paraguayan banks and some foreign banks maintained this system of parallel balance sheets before the crisis to avoid the implicit taxation of the high reserve requirement, as well as the taxation on earning, and to circumvent the limits on lending to related parties (Garcia-Herrero, 1997a ; and Insfran Pelozo, 2000). Moreover, poor management brought about excessive insider lending and high credit concentration.

Financial liberalization was not accompanied by the strengthening of prudential regulations and supervision, resulting in the rapid expansion in the financial sector. Banking regulations did not determine prudential norms for asset classification and did not specify connected lending.[48] The required provisions did not reflect the true risks of banks' assets. In addition, lax licensing requirements and low required capitalization permitted a proliferation of new financial institutions (Shogo and Habermeier, 2002). Each large company or group of companies owned a bank, which in turn owned a finance company. As a result, the number of banks and finance companies almost doubled to 103 in 1995 from 54 in 1988 (Figure 2.5).

---

[47]Appendix 2 summarizes the major developments in the financial sector in Paraguay.

[48]In 1992, regulations on loan-risk classification and provisioning were approved.

**Figure 2.5. Number of Financial Institutions, 1988–2004**

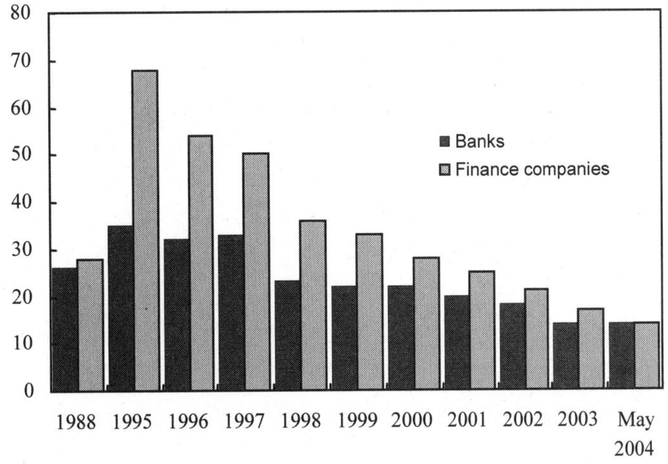

Source: Superintendency of Banks.

Furthermore, the SB lacked adequate powers and resources to exercise effective supervision over the growing number of financial institutions and was constrained by political interference (Shogo and Habermeier, 2002). The authorities acknowledged the insolvency of one-third of the banking system as early as 1989 (Garcia-Herrero, 1997a and b). However, the SB could not take swift corrective measures because of a lack of resources, as well as a weak legal framework and financial regulation and supervision, which did not allow for an easy exit and an efficient resolution of the ailing financial institutions. Political pressure and inadequate documentation, hiding the true situation of banks, also hampered adequate supervision.

## Financial crises

Financial liberalization brought to light vulnerabilities that precipitated the financial sector crisis of 1995–98. Bad banking practices, including excessive concentration and connected lending without the appropriate credit-risk analysis, inadequate accounting practices, and inefficient supervisory framework, triggered the crisis in 1995. Higher interest rates, brought by the financial liberalization, combined with unfavorable terms of trade, further exacerbated the banks' deteriorating balance sheets.[49]

---

[49]Interest rate spreads increased sharply during the months before the crisis. The large spreads not only reflected the implicit tax arising from relatively high reserve requirements, but also the need to cover losses from NPLs, which increased significantly before the crisis (Garcia-Herrero, 1997a).

Notwithstanding a new financial law in 1996, about half of the financial institutions failed between 1995 and 1998. The law required that banks' balance sheets be inspected by external auditors, and authorized banking supervision to intervene in banks that did not comply with prudential regulations or meet the required capital. It also incorporated recommendations set forth by the Basel Committee and created a central risk database. Because the authorities could not take swift measures to clean up the financial sector, the banks' balance sheets worsened.[50] Therefore, the crisis continued in several waves until the end of 1998.

In 2002, fears about the viability of the Argentine-Uruguayan conglomerate Grupo Velox (owners of Banco Alemán, the third-largest bank in Paraguay) led to the closure of the Banco Alemán. The Grupo Velox owned a number of financial and nonfinancial institutions. The Group owned Banco Velox in Argentina; Banco de Montevideo and Banco La Caja Obrera in Uruguay; the Trade and Commercial Bank (TCB), an offshore bank in the Cayman Islands; and several financial institutions in Paraguay, including mutual funds, a finance company, and Banco Alemán, with about 11 percent of banking system assets. The Group had been channeling the deposits captured through its financial institutions in Argentina, Paraguay, and Uruguay to its offshore bank, TCB, which was using them in part to finance the operation of the Group's nonfinancial enterprises. With the financial resources of its Argentine bank frozen and with large exposure to Argentina and Uruguay, the TCB experienced serious liquidity problems and, in mid-May 2002, was unable to satisfy some requests for deposit withdrawals from Paraguayans. The failure to honor TCB commitments intensified the withdrawals from the Group's mutual funds and the Banco Alemán in Paraguay. Between end-2001 and end-July 2002, foreign currency deposits declined by more than US$414 million (33 percent). In June 2002, the authorities intervened and closed Banco Alemán. Because the authorities responded hastily, by end-December 2002 deposits had recovered. Four finance companies also closed in 2002.

The SB intervened in a medium-sized locally owned bank, Multibanco, again in May 2003, after uncovering fraud in this bank. The bank, with around 5 percent of banking system assets, was closed on June 2, 2003. The SB found evidence of irregularities in the bank's lending operations, including connected lending and possible kickbacks paid to attract public sector deposits. As a result of the closure, banking system deposits declined by 7 percent. The authorities moved quickly on Multibanco and began payments under the state deposit guarantee. By

---

[50]The authorities provided liquidity to insolvent banks through a new liquidity-support facility rather than closing them, fearing a systemic financial crisis (Shogo and Habermeier, 2002).

August 2003, deposits had recovered. In 2003, three banks, ING, Asunción, and Paraná, and four finance companies closed because of low profitability.

The crisis in the BNF has eased somewhat, owing to a recapitalization in 2003 and new management, but concerns about its long-term viability remain. Until about mid-2003, the bank had problems clearing its outstanding balances in the payments system. The bank's significant losses have continued to consume its capital. The BNF plays an important role in the payment system (particularly in rural areas) and as a tax and payment agent for the government, which could spark wider problems if the BNF were to close.

## D. Behavior of Private Sector Credit[51]

The latest financial crises combined with political and macroeconomic instability caused private sector credit to decline by about 14 percent in 2002–03 (see Table 2.1). Several factors led to the fall in credit: the government's default on treasury bonds held by banks, the lack of a flexible liquidity support facility at the central bank, the lack of longer-term financing sources, high NPL ratios, high dollarization, and the relative increase of the informal economy.

The closure of four banks in 2003 contributed to the decline of available financing sources. ING, Asunción, Paraná, and Multibanco (together equaling 9.4 percent of the banking system assets) had an outstanding stock of credit of PARG 789 billion by end-2002. About 80 percent of the closed banks' clients have been incorporated in the rest of the banking system.

### Credit supply in banks

The de facto default on the treasury bonds held by the government in December 2002 hurt financial system confidence and contributed to the fall in credit by hitting the net worth of banks. The default on some US$22 million in bonds raised banks' cost of funds. Banks reduced credit lines to both new and current customers as banks started to provision for the defaulted bonds. In October 2003, the new government cleared arrears on domestic bonds through a rollover agreement.

Credit trends started to shift in the region with the onset of the Argentine crisis (Figure 2.6). Credit in Uruguay fell by 25 percent and in Argentina by 15 percent. In Paraguay, wholly foreign-owned banks became more risk averse than local

[51]This section was drawn from discussions with members of the Banks' Association, the private sector, and the authorities, as well as from data analysis.

### Figure 2.6. Private Sector Credit as a Share of GDP in the Region
*(In percent)*

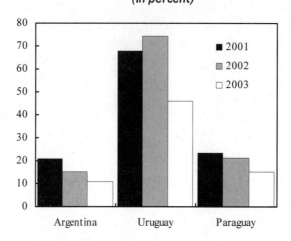

Sources: International Monetary Fund; and Fund staff estimates.

banks as regional uncertainties and the country risk increased after the 2002 crises. According to the Bankers' Association, some wholly foreign-owned banks began implementing sharper supervision following headquarters' instructions and tightening their prudential regulations internally. Wholly foreign-owned banks became more conservative in their lending operations and reduced their liabilities by increasing requirements both on collateral and on new deposit accounts. Other banks have changed their strategy by refocusing on more profitable sectors of the economy—the agricultural and livestock sectors—where solid collateral can be claimed.

Moreover, the lack of a flexible liquidity support facility led banks to accumulate excess liquidity to hedge against a possible deposit run, thus further reducing available funds for private sector lending.[52] The central bank's liquidity support facilities are inadequate. The only facilities available are (1) a short-term liquidity line (call money) for up to 10 days and up to 75 percent of the borrower's capital, collateralized by government bonds, BCP's bills, or first-grade portfolio; and

---

[52]By end-2003, wholly foreign–owned banks held 44 percent of bonds, majority-owned foreign banks held 49 percent, and local banks held 6 percent.

(2) a repurchase agreement of government bonds in open market operations, with financial characteristics that are decided on an ad hoc basis. In addition, as the Central Bank Board of Directors should approve case-by-case each liquidity request and could be legally prosecuted if banks turn out to be insolvent, this facility cannot be used readily. As this serves more as a lender-of-last resort mechanism, as opposed to a short-term liquidity mechanism, banks use it only when they are facing severe liquidity problems. The banks that use this facility are easily labeled by the BCP and by other financial institutions as unsound, because banks that previously used this facility had to be closed subsequently. The interbank money market, which could serve to meet temporary liquidity problems, is very thin, especially now, when all banks are very liquid.

Another factor hindering medium- and long-term credit is the lack of long-term financing sources (Tables 2.2 and 2.3). Although deposits rose by 6 percent in December 2003, the availability of credit has been limited. After the 2002 banking crisis, depositors feared that the government would pursue interventionist policies similar to those seen in Argentina, such as *guaranización* or *corralito* (freezing of deposits), and shifted their savings from longer- to shorter-term deposits. Sight deposits as a share of total deposits increased to 77 percent in 2003 from 67 percent in 2002. To avoid a high maturity mismatch between assets and liabilities, banks in Paraguay restrained from lending at longer terms.

The high stock of NPLs reduced profitability of banks and contributed to the fall in credit supply. Loan performance deteriorated in 2002 as a result of the economic slowdown and currency depreciation (Figure 2.7). Excluding the BNF, the NPL ratio increased from 12.3 percent in December 2001 to 15 percent in December 2003. Returns on assets and equity declined significantly. In addition, the inefficient judicial system became a barrier to the effective resolution of distressed debts, delaying further the recovery of assets.[53]

The lack of hedging instruments against exchange rate volatility, mainly for long-term loans, also contributed to the fall in credit.[54] The high ratio of loans in foreign currency (55 percent), many to borrowers who were not naturally hedged in foreign currency, made the system vulnerable to exchange rate fluctuations. In 2001–03 the total amount of U.S. dollar—denominated credit extended by banks to the private sector contracted by about 40 percent. To avoid exchange rate risks, banks started to lend only to sectors whose revenues were in dollars. Most sectors received their earnings in local currency, except the export-agricultural sector.

---

[53]The recovery of assets can take from three to seven years.

[54]NPL ratio on foreign exchange (23 percent) is higher than on local currency (18 percent).

**Figure 2.7. Nonperforming Loans for Banks**

*(In percent)*

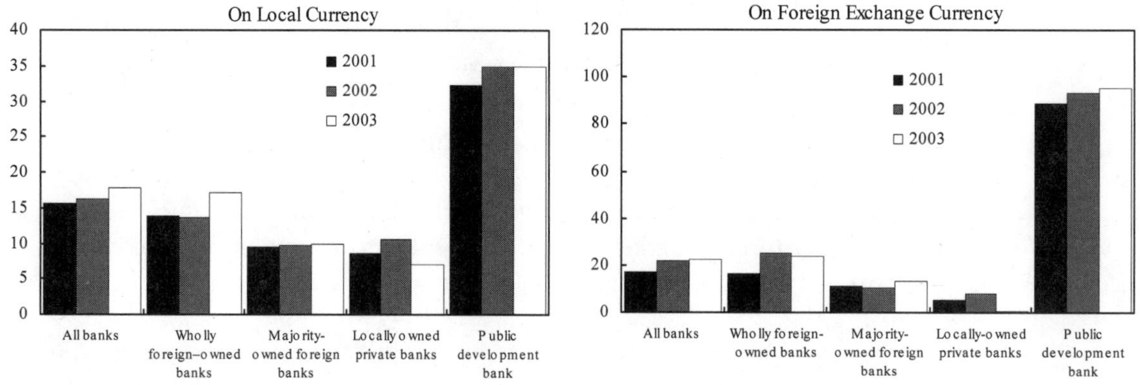

Sources: Superintendency of Banks; and Fund staff estimates.

The large scale of the informal economy contributed to the fall in credit supply. Banks require fiscal balances and cash flows from borrowers. After the 2002 crisis, more people shifted to the informal economy to evade taxation, thus reducing access to bank financing.

### Credit supply in finance companies

Credit supply in finance companies increased in 2003, contrary to the trend in banks (Table 2.1). While deposits increased by 40 percent, credit expanded by 15 percent. In contrast to banks, finance companies hold only 1 percent of the bond stock, leaving the finance companies marginally vulnerable to the bond default. Most of the savings in finance companies are at longer-term maturities (82 percent of total deposits). NPL ratios and profitability are better relative to banks (see Table 2.2). Finance companies are less conservative in lending practices than banks.

### Credit supply in cooperatives

The cooperative sector has increased its lending position by attracting clients who fled from the banking system after the Banco Alemán crisis. The cooperatives can pay more attractive interest rates than other financial institutions because they are exempt from value-added tax (VAT) and from legal reserve requirements. While cooperatives pay 4–8 percent in sight deposits, banks pay 2 percent. Moreover, the higher interest rates on fixed-term deposits in the cooperatives encouraged the public to place their financing in longer-term maturities. Only 23 percent of banking deposits are placed at fixed terms, whereas 60 percent of cooperative deposits are at fixed terms.

## Credit demand

The recession and exchange rate depreciation in 2002 affected most sectors of the economy. Real GDP declined by 2.3 percent, and the exchange rate depreciated by 34 percent in 2002, leading to the collapse of several firms. All sectors of the economy suffered, except for agriculture, because of a good harvest and favorable international prices (Table 2.4). The agricultural corporate sector (particularly, soybean and cotton), with good credit rating, maintained access to banking finances. The agricultural sector, lacking banking access, financed itself through retained earnings or by selling their products on the futures markets. In 2003, credit allocation fell significantly to wholesale commerce (37 percent), to consumption (26 percent), and to industry (14 percent).

The high cost of bank intermediation contributed to low credit demand. Lending interest rates started to fall in 2003, but real interest rates remained high (see Tables 2.2 and 2.5, and Figure 2.8). The interest rate spread between banks and finance companies has shrunk during 2003. Interest rates vary significantly among banks. Locally owned banks, Banco de la Nación Argentina (a wholly foreign-owned bank), and Continental (a majority-owned foreign bank) tend to charge higher interest rates on loans and pay more attractive interest rates on deposits.

The unfavorable business environment discourages investment in Paraguay. According to a World Bank business environment report (World Bank 2004), it is more challenging to open a business in Paraguay than elsewhere in the region.[55] While entrepreneurs in Paraguay must complete 17 steps to launch a business over 74 days on average at a cost equal to about 158 percent of gross national income (GNI) per capita, entrepreneurs in the region need to take 11 steps over 70 days at a lower cost of 60 percent of GNI per capita. The employment laws index, a measure of rigidity in labor regulations and law, is worse in Paraguay (73) compared with the regional average (61) and the **Organization for Economic Co-operation and Development (OECD)** (45). However, credit enforcement complexity in Paraguay is lower than in the region but higher than in the OECD. Similarly, it is time consuming and costly to close a business in Paraguay. Moreover, the lack of property rights protection, the weak legal system, and institutionalized corruption further discourage investment (Gwartney and Lawson, 2003).

---

[55]See Appendix 3 for a comparison of the World Bank Business Environment in Paraguay, the OECD, and the Latin America and Caribbean region.

### Table 2.4. Sectoral Credit Allocation for Banks and Finance Companies

| | 2002 | 2003 | Percentage Change | Sectoral Credit/ Total Bank Credit (In percent) |
|---|---|---|---|---|
| | (In billions of guaraníes) | | | |
| **Total Financial System** | | | | |
| Agriculture | 1,092 | 1,269 | 16.3 | 19.4 |
| Livestock | 273 | 286 | 4.5 | 4.4 |
| Industry | 1,036 | 896 | −13.5 | 13.7 |
| Wholesale commerce | 1,920 | 1,209 | −37.0 | 18.5 |
| Retail commerce | 353 | 427 | 21.0 | 6.5 |
| Services | 1,284 | 1,276 | −0.6 | 19.5 |
| Consumption | 1,581 | 1,179 | −25.5 | 18.0 |
| Export | 32 | 3 | −91.0 | 0.0 |
| **Total** | **7,570** | **6,544** | **−13.5** | **100.0** |
| **Commercial Banks** | | | | |
| Agriculture | 1,056 | 1,226 | 16.1 | 21.7 |
| Livestock | 268 | 280 | 4.7 | 5.0 |
| Industry | 1,020 | 876 | −14.1 | 15.5 |
| Wholesale commerce | 1,761 | 1,154 | −34.5 | 20.4 |
| Retail commerce | 240 | 217 | −9.6 | 3.8 |
| Services | 1,162 | 1,164 | 0.2 | 20.6 |
| Consumption | 1,252 | 728 | −41.8 | 12.9 |
| Export | 31 | 2 | −93.3 | 0.0 |
| **Total** | **6,790** | **5,648** | **−16.8** | **100.0** |
| **Finance Companies** | | | | |
| Agriculture | 36 | 43 | 21.9 | 4.8 |
| Livestock | 6 | 5 | −5.0 | 0.6 |
| Other | 16 | 20 | 25.0 | 2.2 |
| Wholesale commerce | 159 | 55 | −65.5 | 6.1 |
| Retail commerce | 113 | 210 | 85.7 | 23.4 |
| Services | 121 | 112 | −7.7 | 12.5 |
| Consumption | 329 | 450 | 36.8 | 50.2 |
| Export | 0 | 1 | 80.6 | 0.1 |
| **Total** | **780** | **897** | **14.9** | **100.0** |

Source: Superintendency of Banks.

### Table 2.5.  Interest Rates by Banks
*(In percent)*

|  | Commercial Loan >1 Year | Consumption Loan ≤1 Year | Consumption Loan > 1 Year | Sight Deposits | Term Deposits ≤90 Days | Term Deposits ≤365 Days | Certificate of Deposits ≤365 Days |
|---|---|---|---|---|---|---|---|
| ***Wholly foreign–owned banks*** | | | | | | | |
| Citibank N.A. | . . . | . . . | . . . | 2.9 | 1.7 | . . . | 3.9 |
| Lloyds TSB Bank P.L.C. | 25.8 | 34.9 | 32.4 | 3.7 | 5.6 | . . . | 7.3 |
| ABN Amro Bank N.V. | 27.1 | 29.0 | 30.1 | . . . | 2.0 | 6.0 | 6.1 |
| Banco do Brasil S.A. | . . . | 30.6 | 28.1 | 0.7 | . . . | . . . | 2.8 |
| Banco de la Nación Argentina | . . . | 48.2 | . . . | . . . | 7.2 | . . . | 10.3 |
| Chinatrust Commercial Bank | . . . | 32.3 | 31.5 | 1.6 | . . . | . . . | . . . |
| ***Majority-owned foreign banks*** | | | | | | | |
| Interbanco S.A. | 27.6 | 32.7 | 37.2 | 1.9 | 6.0 | . . . | 12.4 |
| Banco Sudameris S.A.E.C.A. | 29.7 | 23.5 | 35.0 | 4.1 | 6.6 | . . . | 12.2 |
| Banco Bilbao Viscaya | | | | | | | |
|    Argentaria Paraguay S.A. | 31.9 | 24.4 | 33.7 | 3.1 | 5.7 | . . . | 6.4 |
| Banco Integración S.A. | 26.8 | 24.5 | 29.7 | 5.1 | . . . | . . . | . . . |
| Banco Continental S.A.E.C.A. | 52.5 | 40.2 | 48.3 | 5.8 | . . . | . . . | 14.5 |
| ***Locally owned private banks*** | | | | | | | |
| Banco Regional S.A. | 45.4 | 41.2 | . . . | 5.9 | 6.3 | 7.2 | 13.4 |
| Banco Amambay S.A. | 48.6 | 48.4 | 37.4 | 3.1 | 15.9 | . . . | . . . |
| ***Public development bank*** | | | | | | | |
| Banco Nacional de Fomento | 29.0 | 28.5 | 49.6 | 5.1 | . . . | . . . | 14.2 |

Source: Superintendency of Banks.

## E. Conclusions and Policy Recommendations

Paraguay has suffered from outbreaks of financial crises since the financial liberalization initiated in the 1990s. The financial crisis that broke out in 1995 did not subside until 1998, after wiping out about half of the banks. The financial sector remained relatively stable until 2002, when a deposit run, caused by the regional outlook, led the authorities to intervene in the third-largest bank and to close four finance companies. In 2003, a locally owned private bank and four more finance companies had to close. Moreover, because of low profit, three banks ceased operations voluntarily.

**Figure 2.8. Lending Interest Rates on Guaraníes**

(*Weighted, in percent*)

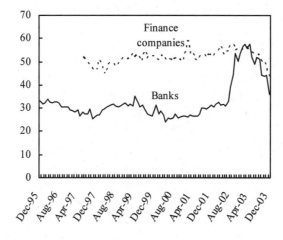

Source: Central Bank of Paraguay.

The origins of the three financial crises can be traced to a weak legal framework and financial supervision. Moreover, the SB has lacked autonomy and resources and has suffered political interference.

The macroeconomic impact of the crises in 1995–98 and 2002 differed from that of the 2003 crisis. In 1998 and 2002, real GDP declined, the exchange rate significantly depreciated, money contracted by about 3 percent, interest rates on central bank bills increased to about 25 percent, and holdings at the BCP grew by about 12 percent (Table 2.1). A better macroeconomic outlook mitigated the spillover effects of the 2003 crisis. The good harvest year and favorable agricultural prices contributed to economic growth and currency appreciation. Money grew by 25 percent, interest rates fell on central bank bills to 13 percent, and holdings at the BCP grew by 44 percent. The risks to the economy from the Multibanco collapse were eased by the bank's relatively small size. Economic agents, foreseeing the bank's fragilities, adjusted their expectations accordingly. Since 2003, however, credit supply has declined significantly.

The authorities have taken key steps to address vulnerabilities in the financial system. By end-2003, a new regulation on asset classification, credit risk, provisioning requirements, and imputation of accrued interest was approved (Resolution 8). This new regulation seeks to bring asset classification and provisioning levels to commonly practiced standards. The gradual implementation of the regulation in 2004–06 will lead to a substantial increase in the level of provisions and thus improve the resilience of financial institutions to shocks. The authorities should coordinate and implement gradually all new and forthcoming financial regulations and laws to avoid a further credit tightening by banks.

The authorities started implementing the financial resolution law, which was approved in 2003. The law expedites the resolution process by addressing some of the difficulties in the financial system. It establishes clear procedures for bank intervention and resolution, and introduces a deposit insurance fund. In particular it (1) creates a permanent deposit insurance fund to protect the general public up to a defined limit per individual; (2) creates a bank recapitalization fund to provide additional public capital support to banks in difficulty and also in case of systemic risk (on a case-by-case basis, within strict guidelines); (3) develops legal tools to allow for the quick transfer of deposits to other financial institutions during bank resolutions; (4) provides adequate legal protection to public officials working in the bank resolution process during the intervention period;[56] and (5) delegates to the BCP the authority to issue regulations related to the deposit guarantee and banking resolution.

With the assistance of the World Bank, the authorities have prepared a Comprehensive Banking Law to strengthen further banking supervision. This law is expected to be approved in 2005 and aims at: (1) upgrading regulatory requirements for risk-weighted capital, (2) bringing accounting and prudential standards up to international best practices, and (3) improving the operational capacity of the SB.

To address weaknesses in the public bank, the authorities prepared a Public Banking Law, which is being discussed in Parliament. The law, prepared with the assistance of the IDB, aims at consolidating several public-lending institutions into a retail bank for microenterprises and small farmers, and a small second-tier bank to on-lend resources from bilateral and multilateral development lenders. The SB should monitor closely the evolution of financial indicators of each financial entity to detect any risks in the system at an early stage, and should forcefully take corrective measures. Supervision could also be strengthened by better coordinating off- and on-site inspections. The authorities should allocate more resources to the SB to improve information systems, training, and incentives.

---

[56]Public official workers can be prosecuted after the resolution process, precluding them from carrying out their tasks adequately.

Paraguay will benefit from the thorough assessment of its financial sector through the Financial System Assessment Program (FSAP) that is jointly undertaken by the IMF and the World Bank, and that will be concluded by mid-2005.[57] The FSAP identifies strengths, risks, and vulnerabilities of the financial system; assesses observance of financial system standards, codes, and good practices; determines how key sources of risk are being managed; ascertains the financial system's developmental and technical assistance needs; and helps prioritize financial system policies to meet these needs.

The authorities should move forward with the reform agenda, increasing tax and customs efficiency, tackling governance issues, and reforming the judicial system. It is crucial that the government not fall into arrears or default on treasury bonds again. The rollover agreement on the defaulted bonds in 2003 was a stepping-stone to help banks increase their confidence in the government's repayment commitment and accelerate the engine of intermediation in the long run. The authorities should pursue tax and customs reforms to help formalize the informal economy, thus increasing the potential of borrowers with improved conditions to access credit. Better management of the social security institute's (IPS) funds would help finance longer-term projects. The authorities should enhance the BCP's liquidity-support facilities in such a way that they become readily and automatically available if needed, and should deepen the interbank market. They should reform the judicial system to improve the investment climate.

In the long run, political, economic, and financial stability will improve depositors' and financial institutions' confidence, helping restart the engine of growth. By pursuing a sound macroeconomic policy, the authorities will give a positive signal to the financial sector and will help reduce the country's risk in the long run, allowing wholly foreign-owned banks to resume lending. Political consensus is of paramount importance to push forward with economic reforms and will contribute to building confidence and credibility. The stability will allow depositors to place their funds at longer-term maturities and to invest in the country. At the same time, financial institutions will facilitate intermediation, stimulating productive investment and growth.

## References

Ashwell, Washington, 2000, "La Crisis Financiera del Paraguay," *Boletin del CEMLA* (July–August), pp. 170–74.

---

[57]The SB has benefited from the numerous technical assistance missions on financial supervision and regulation from the Monetary and Financial Systems Department of the IMF since 1994.

Creane, Susan, Rishi Goyal, Mushfiq Mobarak, Randa Sab, 2004, "Financial Sector Development in the Middle East and North Africa," IMF Working Paper 04/201 (Washington: International Monetary Fund).

Gwartney, James, and Robert Lawson, with Neil Emerick, 2003, *Economic Freedom of the World: 2003 Annual Report* (Vancouver: The Fraser Institute and the Economic Freedom Network).

Gamarra, Regis, 2004a, "Fuerte Crecimiento," *Enfoque Económico* (May).

————, 2004b, "Las Cooperativas Más Grandes," *Enfoque Económico* (April).

Garcia-Herrero, Alicia, 1997a, "Banking Crises in Latin America in the 1990s: Lessons from Argentina, Paraguay, and Venezuela," IMF Working Paper 97/140 (Washington: International Monetary Fund).

————, 1997b, "Monetary Impact of Banking and the Conduct of Monetary Policy," IMF Working Paper 97/124 (Washington: International Monetary Fund).

Insfran Pelozo, Anibal, 1999, "Concentración de Depósitos, Tamaño de los Bancos y Sus Efectos Sobre la Oferta de Crédito para las Empresas. El Caso Paraguayo," paper presented at the Catholic University "Nuestra Señora de la Asunción "(July).

————, 2000, "El Sistema Financiero Paraguayo. Evaluando 10 Años de Transición," paper presented at the 22nd International Congress Association of Latin American Studies, (Miami) March.

Penner, Reinaldo, 1994, "Financial Liberalization in an Agrarian Economy: The Case of Paraguay," in *Financial System Reforms, Economic Growth, and Stability* (Washington: World Bank).

Shogo, Ishii, and Karl Habermeier, 2002, *Capital Account Liberalization and Financial System Stability*, IMF Occasional Paper No. 211 (Washington: International Monetary Fund).

Straub, Stéphane, 1998, "Evolución Macroeconómica del Paraguay 1989–1997: Burbuja de Consumo y Crisis Financiera," *Revista de la Cepal*, Vol. 65, pp. 119–32.

Transparency International, 2003. Available via the Internet: http://www.transparency.org/

World Bank, 2004, "Doing Business: Benchmarking Business Regulations." Available via the Internet: http://rru.worldbank.org/DoingBusiness/default.aspx.

# 1    Analysis of the Financial System

## Financial Liberalization and Monetary Policy

**History of financial liberalization**

Before the 1990s, interest rates were subject to administrative controls, the banking law limited banks' operations, reserve requirements ratios were very high (42 percent), credit allocation was determined by law, the BCP financed agricultural exports through the rediscount papers, the exchange rate was fixed, and public sector funds were deposited at the central bank.

Around 1989, the foreign exchange market and interest rates were liberalized. Reserve requirements were reduced, the rediscount papers at the BCP were gradually eliminated, and norms for asset classification were legislated.

From 1990 to 1993, more reforms were implemented. Among them were further reductions in reserve requirements and freeing of public sector deposits from the BCP to the banking system.

**Monetary policy objective**

From 1999 to 2003, monetary policy lacked focus. The BCP attempted to pursue multiple targets, sometimes focusing on the exchange rate, at other times pursuing monetary or inflation objectives. Monetary management was complicated in early 2003 by political pressures to extend US$39 million in credit to the government and an attempt by the Ministry of Finance to use public sector deposits to manage monetary policy. In early 2004, the BCP extended a US$33 million advance loan to help the central government pay external arrears. With the approval of a monetary program by end-2003, the monetary authorities have pursued a monetary policy geared mainly toward achieving the inflation target of the program.

**Commonly used monetary policy tools**

Open market operations through central bank bills, which are issued daily at terms ranging upward from 35 days and are fully negotiable up to 360 days, or through call money, with terms from 1 to 15 days. Changes in reserve requirements are used less frequently. This was used more in 2002 after excess liquidity in the system drove the BCP to change its rates.

## Direct Monetary Policy Instruments

**Interest rate liberalization status**

Interest rates are liberalized. However, to avoid aggressive competition, banks cannot offer rates higher than 50 percent of the effective weighted average on deposits. In 2003, legislation setting limits on credit card interest rates was approved; however, it was declared unconstitutional.

**Credit controls**

There are no credit controls.

**Bank-by-bank ceilings**

There are no ceilings.

| | |
|---|---|
| Directed credits | The government supports the agricultural system, mainly, the soy, cotton, and wheat campaigns, by taking ad hoc monetary policy measures that benefit these systems; for instance, reducing reserve requirements on banking deposits if banks lend to productive systems. |

## Indirect Monetary Policy Instruments

| | |
|---|---|
| Reserve requirements | Reserve requirement rates remained constant from 1994 until June 2002, when excess liquidity in the banking system drove the BCP to increase the rates, lowering them again in November 2002. |
| Required-reserve ratio (domestic currency) | Demand deposits (less than 30 days): 15 percent. Term deposits (30–180 days): 15 percent. Term deposits (181–360 days): 15 percent. Term deposits (361–540 days): 7 percent. Term deposits (more than 540 days): 0 percent. |
| Required-reserve ratio (foreign currency) | Demand deposits (less than 30 days): 26.5 percent. Term deposits (30–360 days): 26.5 percent. Term deposits (361–540 days): 16.5 percent. Term deposits (541–1,080 days): 6.5 percent. Term deposits (more than 1080 days): 1.5 percent. |
| Discount window | This facility is not very flexible and does not adequately address temporary liquidity problems of banks. It is usually used when the bank is facing severe liquidity problems. However, in most cases, the banks that used this facility ended up being insolvent and had to close. Although the central bank has in the past used medium-term liquidity support facilities to help ailing banks, the legal actions against BCP directors that ensued prevent de facto their use. The only facilities available are (1) a short-term liquidity line (call money) for up to 10 days and 75 percent of the borrower's capital, collateralized by government bonds, BCP's bills, or first-grade portfolio; and (2) a repurchase agreement of government bonds in open market operations, with financial characteristics that are decided on an ad hoc basis. In addition, the process is cumbersome, as the Central Bank Board of Directors on a case-by-case basis should approve each liquidity request. |
| Open market operations | The most widely used monetary policy tools are open market operations through central bank bills, which are issued daily at maturities ranging upward from 35 days and are fully negotiable up to 360 days, or through call money, with maturities from 1 to 15 days. This is the most active instrument, and the BCP has increased its stock of bills significantly during 2003. More recently, owing to the high quasi-fiscal cost, the BCP has been reducing the issuance of the bills by limiting them to longer-term maturities. |

## Treasury Bonds

| | |
|---|---|
| Treasury bonds market | Treasury bonds exist. However, the placement of these bonds has been very difficult; in particular, they became illiquid owing to the de facto default on the treasury bonds by the government in December 2002. In October 2003, the government cleared arrears on domestic bonds with banks by restructuring the debt. As these bonds are not liquid, they are not traded in a secondary market. Treasury bonds are held by contractuals and suppliers, who in turn negotiate them with banks. |

## Banking System

| | |
|---|---|
| Number of banks | 14 banks (6 wholly foreign-owned banks; 5 majority-owned foreign banks; 2 locally owned private banks; 1 public bank). |
| Size of banking system | 72 percent of financial assets. |
| Number of public banks | One public bank, Banco Nacional del Fomento. Besides the BNF, there are seven public entities that channel subsidized funds, mainly from the international donor community. Five (CAH, FG, FDC, BANAVI, CONAVI) of these seven entities are first-tier institutions, whereas the other two (UTEP, FDI) are second-tier institutions. |
| Public bank assets as a share of total assets in the banking system | 8 percent. |
| Strategy for restructuring the public banks | The Public Banking Law aims at consolidating several public lending institutions into a retail bank for microenterprises and small farmers, and a small second-tier bank to on-lend resources from bilateral and multilateral development lenders. In the interim, the National Development Bank has been recapitalized and its operations are being modernized and streamlined. |
| Lending limits on the public bank | There are limits on BNF loans. One-year loans are limited to PARG100 million per corporation, three-year loans to PARG300 million, and loans with maturity greater than five years to PARG700 million. |
| Interbank transactions | There is an interbank money market, but it is very thin, especially now, when all banks are very liquid. |
| Noncash transactions | Cash and ATM cards are widely used. Credit cards are not yet widely used, given the informality of the economy. Moreover, interest rates on credit cards are very high. Although the economy is highly dollarized, dollars are not commonly used in transactions. |

## Financial Regulation and Supervision

| | |
|---|---|
| Financial regulation and supervision | Financial supervision of banks, finance companies, savings and loans associations, exchange houses, warehouses, and public entities is carried out by the Superintendency of Banks (SB), an institution that is part of the BCP, according to the financial law 489/95. The SB is divided into four units: administrative, special supervision, inspection, and financial analysis and regulations. The SB has 160 employees. Nearly 40 percent of the personnel of the SB are devoted to Special Supervision, the unit in charge of liquidation of banks, leaving a reduced group to work in the area of preventive supervision. Supervisors in the SB need additional training in the more sophisticated and forward-looking components of credit risk assessment, such as cash flow analysis and the assessment of borrower's capacity to pay. |
| Banking and finance companies' average capital-asset ratio | Minimum capital risk-weighted assets ratio is 10 percent. |

| | |
|---|---|
| Entry of financial institutions | Entry of banks is easy. The required minimum capital for banks is PARG10 billion and for finance companies, PARG5 billion, which are adjusted annually to the consumer price index (CPI). |
| Exit of financial institutions | Exit of banks is easy. Banks can wind down operations voluntarily. |
| Deposit insurance | Paraguay had a state deposit guarantee. The scheme was not funded and depended on disbursements from the BCP. The level of covered deposits reflected 75 minimum wages. By end-2003, a Bank Resolution Law was approved, which created a deposit insurance fund to protect the public up to a defined limit per individual. |
| Central bank borrower database | Yes. |
| Data collection | Detailed data collected regularly on a monthly basis. |
| Limits on exposure to single borrowers or related borrowers | The limit on the loans is 20 percent of the bank's capital, rising to 30 percent for loans to other financial institutions. |
| Inspection and auditing | Banks and finance companies publish a general balance sheet and income statement, which are audited by external auditors, within 120 days of each fiscal year. The SB publishes the CADEF, a composite rating system that describes the financial situation of each entity, four times a year. |
| Payment system | There is no electronic payment system. Checks play a dominant role as both payment instrument and a way to settle outstanding obligations among banks. The checks are cleared at the Clearing House for checks, which itself settles manually over the banks' current accounts at the BCP. The Clearing House consists only of a paper- and manual-handling procedure, and it lacks normal safety and efficiency requirements for clearinghouses. The BCP is receiving technical assistance from the IMF in this area. |

## Other Financial Entities

| | |
|---|---|
| Finance companies | There were 17 finance companies by end-2003, accounting for about 7 percent of financial assets. In 2004, the number dropped to 14. |
| Mortgage market | There is a first-tier public entity for housing, called Banco Nacional de la Vivienda (BNV). Related to the BNV is the Consejo Nacional de la Vivienda (CONAVI), which oversees BNV operations and also acts as a second-tier lender for housing investments. |
| Stock market | Paraguay's first stock market began trading in October 1993. Companies have a minimum paid-up capital of US$50,000. In 2002, trading was only US$12 million, significantly lower than the US$15.5 million traded in 2001. |
| Sovereign/corporate debt | Corporate debt is limited. Sovereign debt is mostly multilateral on a concessional basis. |
| Pension funds | There is a pay-as-you-go social security public pension system, the caja fiscal, for public employees and IPS for private employees. |

| | |
|---|---|
| Mutual funds | Mutual funds are very limited. |
| Insurance companies | There are 35 insurance companies. The system is regulated by the Superintendencia de Seguros. Since March 1998, insurance companies must have a minimum paid-up capital of US$500,000, substantially consolidating the insurance market. |
| Money exchange houses | There are 23 money exchange houses, which are supervised by the SB. |
| Cooperatives | Cooperatives account for 20 percent of financial assets. |
| Deposit warehouses | Four deposit warehouses, which are supervised by the SB. |

## Institutional and Legal Environment

| | |
|---|---|
| Institutional/legal environment | There are serious governance issues in most institutions. In addition, the government sometimes takes ad hoc measures that bring uncertainties to bankers. |
| Loan recovery through judicial system | It takes between three and seven years to conclude a judicial process. |
| Country risk rating (EIU) | Overall Rating: D. Total score: 66 (as of 2/2004) <br> Political Risk: E <br> Economic Policy: C <br> Economic Structure: D <br> Liquidity Risk: D |
| Country's ratings (Standard & Poor's and Moody's) | On February 13, 2003, Standard & Poor's downgraded Paraguayan foreign currency debt to SD (Selective Default), owing to nonpayment of domestic bonds held by banks. On April 29, 2003, Moody's significantly downgraded the country ceiling for foreign currency bonds and notes to Caa1 from B2, and the country ceiling for foreign currency bank deposits to Caa2 from B3. At the time, this rating reflected Moody's concern that a bank deposit run in Paraguay might coincide with or presage a default on the nation's debt. The 2004 Moody's report maintained these ratings. |
| Central bank independence | The charter of the BCP states that it is a technical body endowed with administrative, financial, and regulatory autonomy limited by the constitution and the laws. However, financial autonomy is curtailed by the fact that BCP's budget is part of the national budget and the annual government budget law. This impairs the BCP's actual financial independence and is a potentially severe limitation of its ability to conduct policy independently. In February 2004, the Ministry of Finance and the central bank signed a memorandum of understanding that will grant the bank greater operational autonomy. |
| Information dissemination in the central bank website | Well-maintained website. Monetary and financial data are well disseminated. Financial legislation and resolutions are posted in the BCP website. |
| Fund documents publication | Yes. Fund documents published on the website. |
| IMF programs | Latest Stand-By Arrangement was approved in December 2003. There were also arrangements in 1957, 1958, 1959, 1960, 1961, 1964, 1966, 1968, and 1969. |

## Financial System Openness and Exchange Rate

| | |
|---|---|
| Restrictions on purchase/sale of financial assets by foreigners | Free from restrictions. |
| Restrictions on purchase of foreign currency by residents | Free from restrictions. |
| Repatriation requirements | Free from restrictions. |
| Exchange rate regime | Floating exchange rate; however, to maintain a stable real exchange rate, the authorities sometimes intervene in the market. |
| Article VIII/XIV status | VIII. Date of acceptance: August 23, 1994. |
| Multiple exchange rates | Free from restrictions. |
| Parallel exchange market | Free from restrictions. |
| Forward exchange market | Banks are permitted to enter into forward transactions with respect to trade transactions and on terms that may be negotiated freely with customers. |

# 2   Major Financial Sector Developments in Paraguay

| Dates | Developments |
|---|---|
| 1989–1994 | Financial liberalization process. |
| 1995, 1997, 1998 | Financial crises because of a lack of adequate bank regulation and supervision, inadequate banking skills, poor credit and risk assessment, and high levels of insider lending and loan concentration. |
| June 2002 | Intervention in the country's third-largest bank, Banco Alemán, with about 11 percent of banking system assets. |
| December 2002 | Default on domestic bonds held by the banking system. |
| January 2003 | Decree announcing the transfer of public sector deposits from banks to the BCP. |
| May 2003 | Intervention in a medium-sized domestic bank, Multibanco, with around 5 percent of banking system assets. |
| August 2003 | New administration. |
| October 2003 | The president signed a political agreement with the heads of both houses of Congress and with opposition party leaders to pass a series of economic reform laws, including fiscal adjustment legislation and laws to strengthen the banking system and reorganize public banks, reform the public employees' pension plan, restructure public enterprises, and pass a new customs code. |
| November 2003 | Approval of stricter regulations on asset classification, credit risk, provisioning requirements, and imputation of accrued interest (Resolution 8) seeks to bring asset classification and provisioning levels to standard international practice. |
| December 2003 | Approval of a bank resolution law.<br><br>Approval of a Stand-By Arrangement to help the government create conditions for sustained economic growth and poverty reduction and address long-standing governance problems. The program includes fiscal consolidation, clearance of arrears, the strengthening of the financial system, increased autonomy of the BCP, and structural reforms to address the long-standing governance issues by improving the efficiency and transparency of government operations. |

# 3

# Snapshot of Business Environment

The tables below provide a snapshot of the business climate in Paraguay by identifying specific regulations and policies that encourage or discourage investment, productivity, and growth. Key indicators are used to help measure the ease or difficulty of operating a business: starting a business, hiring and firing workers, enforcing contracts, getting credit, and closing a business. Regional and OECD averages are provided for each topic for comparison.

## Snapshot of Business Environment—Paraguay

### Starting a business (2004)

The challenges of launching a business in Paraguay are shown below through four measures: procedures required to establish a business, the associated time, the cost, and the minimum capital requirement. Entrepreneurs can expect to go through 17 steps to launch a business over 74 days on average, at a cost equal to 157.6 percent of gross national income per capita. There is no minimum deposit requirement to obtain a business registration number, compared with the regional average of 32.3 percent of GNI and the OECD average of 47.0 percent of GNI.

| Indicator | Paraguay | Regional Average | OECD Average |
|---|---|---|---|
| Number of procedures | 17 | 11 | 6 |
| Duration (days) | 74 | 70 | 25 |
| Cost (percent of GNI per capita) | 157.6 | 60.1 | 8.4 |
| Minimum capital (percent GNI per capita) | 0.0 | 32.3 | 47.0 |

### Hiring and firing workers (2003)

The flexibility or rigidity of labor regulations and laws in Paraguay is shown below, using three indices. Conditions covered by the indices include availability of part-time and fixed-term contracts, working-time requirements, minimum wage laws, and minimum conditions of employment. Each index assigns values between 0 and 100, with higher values representing more rigid regulations. The overall Employment Laws Index is an average of the three indices. For Paraguay, the overall index is 73, compared with the regional average of 61 and OECD average of 45.

| Indicator | Paraguay | Regional Average | OECD Average |
|---|---|---|---|
| Flexibility of hiring index | 58 | 56 | 49 |
| Conditions of employment index | 90 | 79 | 58 |
| Flexibility of firing index | 71 | 48 | 28 |
| Employment laws index | 73 | 61 | 45 |

## Enforcing contracts (2003)

The ease or difficulty of enforcing commercial contracts in Paraguay is measured below, using three indicators: the number of procedures counted from the moment the plaintiff files a lawsuit until actual payment, the associated time, and the cost (in court and attorney fees). An overall index of the procedural complexity of contract enforcement is calculated by averaging four subindices related to dispute resolution. The index varies from 0 to 100, with higher values indicating more complexity in enforcing a contract. The procedural complexity index for Paraguay is 67, compared with the regional average of 70 and the OECD average of 49.

| Indicator | Paraguay | Regional Average | OECD Average |
|---|---|---|---|
| Number of procedures | 46 | 33 | 18 |
| Duration (days) | 188 | 363 | 213 |
| Cost (percent GNI per capita) | 34.0 | 38.0 | 7.1 |
| Procedural complexity index | 67 | 70 | 49 |

## Getting credit (2003)

Two sets of measures on getting credit in Paraguay are constructed: indicators on credit information sharing and an indicator of the legal protection of creditor rights. A public credit registry index covers credit information coverage, distribution, access, and quality for public registries. The index ranges from 0 to 100. Higher values indicate that the rules are better designed to support credit transactions. For private credit registries, a coverage indicator is reported. An indicator of creditor rights in insolvency is also provided. A minimum score of

0 represents weak creditor rights and a maximum score of 4 represents strong creditor rights. Paraguay has a score of 2, compared with the regional average of 1 and OECD average of 1.

| Indicator | Paraguay | Regional Average | OECD Average |
|---|---|---|---|
| Has public credit registry? | Yes | | |
| Public credit registry (year est.) | 1995 | | |
| Public credit registry coverage (borrowers per 1,000 capita) | .. | 53.2 | 43.2 |
| Public credit registry index | .. | 50 | 58 |
| Has private dredit bureau? | Yes | | |
| Private bureau coverage (borrowers per 1,000 capita) | .. | 196.6 | 443.5 |
| Creditor rights index | 2 | 1 | 1 |

## Closing a business (2003)

The ability of courts to resolve insolvencies in Paraguay is shown below. A goals of insolvency index is calculated by averaging the cost and time associated with resolving an insolvency, the observance of absolute priority of claims, and the outcome (reorganizing viable companies and closing down unviable ones, for example). The goals of insolvency index ranges from 0 to 100. Higher values indicate a more efficient insolvency system. The goals of insolvency index for Paraguay is 46, compared with the regional average of 46 and OECD average of 77. An indicator of the power of the courts during the insolvency process is also provided. A higher value indicates more court involvement in the process, usually an impediment to insolvency resolution. Paraguay has a value of 67, compared with the regional average of 63 and OECD average of 36.

| Indicator | Paraguay | Regional Average | OECD Average |
|---|---|---|---|
| Actual time (in years) | 3.9 | 3.7 | 1.8 |
| Actual cost (percent of estate) | 8 | 15 | 7 |
| Goals of insolvency index | 46 | 46 | 77 |
| Court powers endex | 67 | 63 | 36 |

Source: World Bank.

# 3   Assessing the Reform of the Caja Fiscal

## A. Background

Paraguay's existing pension system is fragmented into eight independent public institutions. Few workers—less than 10 percent of the active labor force—participate in a pension system; 95 percent of pension coverage is provided by two institutions, the Instituto de Previsión Social, which covers private sector employees, and the caja fiscal, which covers public employees (public administration employees, teachers, university professors, police officers, army officers, and judicial employees).[58] These institutions operate as defined benefit pay-as-you-go plans, that is, the pension benefits are financed in principle by the contributions paid by the active workers who participate in the pension plan. In addition to the contributing plans for public employees, the caja fiscal pays noncontributory pension benefits to Chaco War veterans and their survivors.

In recent years, the caja fiscal has generated large deficits, causing serious concerns about its long-term fiscal sustainability. In 2002, the deficit amounted to 1.9 percent of GDP, about 60 percent of which was due to Chaco War pensions. The deficit was somewhat smaller in 2003, 1.5 percent of GDP, because the year-end bonus was not paid as a result of a new law passed by Congress. Retirement ages as low as 40 and high replacement rates, applied on the last wage, contributed to boosting these deficits. Lack of transparency, especially regarding the legitimacy of Chaco War pensions, exacerbated the generosity of the system. Although systematic evidence is not available, anecdotal evidence suggests widespread fraud, possibly on the order of 30 to 40 percent of claims.

---

[58]Other, smaller institutions cover railroad workers, elected Congress officials, employees of the publicly owned electricity company, banks, and municipalities. See World Bank (2003) for a more detailed description of the pension systems in Paraguay and Oficina Internacional del Trabajo (2003) for an actuarial study of the pension system for private sector employees.

The purpose of this chapter is to assess the long-term fiscal implications of the reform of the caja fiscal recently approved by Congress. As part of its reform program, Paraguay's government committed to undertaking a wide-ranging overhaul of the caja fiscal. In particular, the government committed to reform key parameters, such as the contribution rate, the minimum retirement age, and the replacement rates, to ensure the long-term viability of the caja fiscal. Furthermore, as part of its more general anticorruption and transparency campaign, the government also committed to conducting an in-depth review of the registry of the beneficiaries, with the aim of purging it of illegitimate claims. Although we recognize the utmost importance of improving transparency, this chapter focuses on the long-term quantitative impact of the parametric reform of the caja fiscal. As is common in studies that make projections far into the future—our projections extend to 2050—we recommend some caution in interpreting the findings.

Our main finding is that the reform brings about major savings but leaves large unfunded liabilities that will require further reform in the future. The reform addresses explosive dynamics—prior to the reform, the net present value of deficits over 2003–50 reached almost 90 percent of GDP in 2003. However, the reform leaves large unfunded liabilities, in the form of a large net present value of deficits, of about half the prereform scenario, mostly arising from the caja fiscal's main three contributing plans (for teachers, the army, and the police). As a result, ensuring the financial equilibrium of the caja fiscal over the long run will require further reform in the future.

This chapter is organized as follows. Section B describes the main features of the reform approved by Congress relative to the existing regime. Section C discusses our assumptions and methodology for the actuarial calculations. Section D presents our findings. Finally, Section E draws the main policy implications of our study.

## B. Reform of the Caja Fiscal

Both the contributing plans and the Chaco War pensions contributed to the large deficit of the caja fiscal in 2003 (Table 3.1). Specifically:

- The caja fiscal as a whole generated an operational deficit—defined as the difference between annual contributions and annual disbursements— of 1.5 percent of GDP. The six contributing plans and the Chaco War pensions accounted for 55 and 45 percent of this deficit, respectively.[59]

---

[59]The six contributing plans of the caja fiscal cover teachers, public administration employees, university professors, police officers, army officers, and judicial employees.

### Table 3.1. Caja Fiscal in 2003

| | Contributions | | | Disbursements | | | Operational Balance[1] | | |
|---|---|---|---|---|---|---|---|---|---|
| | Active Employees | Millions of guaraníes | Percent of GDP | Pension Recipients | Millions of guaraníes | Percent of GDP | Depen-dency ratio[2] | Millions of guaraníes | Percent of GDP |
| Caja Fiscal | 144,537 | 352,782 | 0.94 | 55,167 | 906,533 | 2.43 | — | −553,750 | −1.48 |
| Contributing plans[3] | 144,537 | 352,782 | 0.94 | 32,132 | 659,977 | 1.77 | 0.22 | −307,195 | −0.82 |
| Public administration | 32,502 | 68,498 | 0.18 | 7,785 | 113,750 | 0.30 | 0.24 | −45,252 | −0.12 |
| Army | 13,738 | 30,565 | 0.08 | 6,813 | 181,259 | 0.49 | 0.50 | −150,694 | −0.40 |
| Police | 15,524 | 35,718 | 0.10 | 3,556 | 96,868 | 0.26 | 0.23 | −61,151 | −0.16 |
| University professors | 10,965 | 18,156 | 0.05 | 522 | 14,095 | 0.04 | 0.05 | 4,061 | 0.01 |
| Judicial employees | 8,546 | 30,122 | 0.08 | 441 | 11,256 | 0.03 | 0.05 | 18,866 | 0.05 |
| Teachers | 63,262 | 169,723 | 0.45 | 13,015 | 242,749 | 0.65 | 0.21 | −73,025 | −0.20 |
| Chaco War veterans | — | — | — | 23,035 | 246,555 | 0.66 | — | −246,555 | −0.66 |
| Veterans | — | — | — | 7,621 | 99,073 | 0.27 | — | −99,073 | −0.27 |
| Survivors | — | — | — | 15,414 | 147,482 | 0.40 | — | −147,482 | −0.40 |

Sources: Ministry of Finance; and Fund staff estimates.

[1]Difference between contributions and disbursements.
[2]Ratio between number of pension recipients (including beneficiaries of survivor pensions) and active employees.
[3]Disbursements include survivor pensions.

- The dependency ratio—defined as the ratio of pension recipients to active employees—for the contributing plans as a whole stood at 0.22, implying that there were, on average, about 4.5 active workers per pension recipient. However, this ratio varied dramatically across plans, ranging from 0.50 for army officers to 0.05 for judicial employees and university professors.

- The plans for army officers and teachers accounted for one-half and one-fourth of the overall deficit of the contributing plans, respectively. As regards army officers, contributions were especially low, covering only about half of the disbursements.

- The plans for university professors and judicial employees were the only ones in surplus. However, these are the smallest plans, both in number of active employees and amount of contributions.

- As regards the Chaco War pensions, disbursements to survivors accounted for almost two-thirds of total disbursements, with disbursements to veterans accounting for the rest.

Congress approved a new law reforming the caja fiscal on December 22, 2003. The new law,[60] with administrative regulations issued on January 30, 2004, aims at improving the actuarial balance of the system and at reducing heterogeneity across old-age pension plans. However, Congress retained a few exceptions, most notably for teachers but also for the police and army plans. As regards the six contributing plans of the caja fiscal, the new law modifies the existing regime by (Table 3.2):

- Increasing the contribution rate from 14 to 16 percent for all pension plans.[61]

- Increasing the retirement age to 62, making retirement mandatory at this age, except for police and army officers—for whom the old rules continue to apply—and teachers. Early retirement is allowed at 50 with at least 20 years of service.

- Broadening in the base wage used to compute the pension benefit by defining it as the average wage in the last five years of service rather than the last wage.[62]

- Defining the replacement rate as 20 percent of the base wage plus 2.7 percent for each year of service (previously 93 percent of the base wage).[63]

- Eliminating the 13-month bonus (*aguinaldo*).

- Limiting pension indexation to consumer price index (CPI) inflation rather than to public wage increases.[64]

The new law retains special provisions for the teachers' pension plan, most important by allowing ordinary retirement after 25 years of service at a replacement rate of 83 percent. These exceptions were negotiated with teachers' unions following strong protests from teachers. Furthermore, the new law introduced a transitory regime that allowed teachers with at least 20 years of service at the time of approval of the new law to opt for the old regime until December 31, 2004 (about 6,000 teachers were eligible).

---

[60]Law 2345/2003.

[61]Article 1 also says that this rate will be maintained until the system achieves financial sustainability.

[62]Furthermore, the law does not require that past wages be adjusted for inflation for the purpose of computing the base wage.

[63]This schedule applies only after 10 years of service. In case of early retirement, the replacement rate is further reduced by multiplying the ratio of the years of service to 62.

[64]If wages increase by less than the inflation rate, pension adjustment is limited to wage increases.

### Table 3.2. Comparison Between the Preexisting Law and the New Law Regulating the Caja Fiscal

| | Old Law | New Law | Comments |
|---|---|---|---|
| **I. General provisions** | | | |
| Contribution rate | 14 percent. | 16 percent. | New rate has to remain effective at least until financial balance is achieved. |
| Contribution base | Base salary. | All taxable remunerations, including base salary, overtime, representation charges, bonuses. | The remuneration base excludes family subsidy and health care contributions. |
| Ordinary retirement age (*jubilación obligatoria*) | Between 40 and 50 years depending on occupation, gender, and years of service. | 62 years. | Retirement is compulsory at age 62. Employees with less than 10 years of service receive 90 percent of their inflation-adjusted contributions. The new rules do not affect police and army officers. |
| Early retirement age (*jubilación*) | Retirement age can be moved forward through various mechanisms. | 50 years of age. | Early retirement is possible with at least 20 years of service. |
| Replacement rate | 93 percent (lower for early retirement). Between 50 and 100 percent depending on years of service, for police and army officers. | 20 percent plus 2.7 percent per each year of service. | The replacement rate reaches its maximum at 100 percent after 40 years of service. In case of early retirement, the replacement rate is multiplied by the the ratio of the age at retirement and 62. The new rules do not affect police and army officers. |
| Base wage for computing pension benefit (*Remuneración base*) | Last wage. | Average wage in last five years of service. | Past wages are not adjusted for inflation in the computation of the base wage. |
| Pension adjustment for inflation | Based on wage increase of working cohort. | Based on average public wage increase but limited to CPI inflation. | The adjustment to Chaco War pensions is determined in the budget law. |
| Thirteenth-month bonus (*aguinaldo*) | Customarily paid but not mandated by law. | Prohibited. | The prohibition applies to all beneficiaries, including Chaco War pensions. |

### Table 3.2 *(concluded)*

|  | Old Law | New Law | Comments |
|---|---|---|---|
| **II. Special provisions for teachers** | | | |
| Ordinary retirement | 45 or 40 years of age for males and females, respectively, with at least 25 years of service. Female teachers can count up to five children as years of service. | At least 28 years of service, or at least 25 years of service at a lower replacement rate. Female teachers can count up to three children as years of service. | |
| Early retirement | 20 years of service (for causes preventing ordinary retirement). | Between 15 and 24 years of service (only for physical or mental incapacity). | |
| Replacement rate | 93 percent (lower for early retirement). | 87 percent; 83 percent for at least 25 years of service. | |
| Base wage for computing pension benefit | Last wage. | Average wage in last five years of service (or 10 years in case of an increase in hours or shifts worked). | Past wages are not adjusted for inflation. |

Sources: Ministry of Finance; and Fund staff analyses.

The new provisions for teachers are nonetheless an improvement over the existing situation. First, the new minimum retirement age for teachers is still higher than the age at which many teachers now retire. Second, the new definition of base wage is particularly important for teachers, given the common current practice of teachers working more hours and shifts just prior to retirement. Finally, the law essentially eliminates early retirement for teachers, which remains only as a disability pension.

The new law also retains important exceptions for army and police officers. The new minimum retirement age and the associated replacement rate do not apply to them; they are allowed to retire using the graduated replacement rates under the old law. Importantly, however, the base wage will be computed using the new law, that is, the replacement rate will be applied to the average wage in the last five years of service rather than to the last wage.

Finally, the law aims at generating savings from the Chaco War pensions. In particular, the law reduces survivor pensions to 75 percent of the original pension (from 100 percent), tightens somewhat the eligibility criteria, and abolishes aguinaldo. Furthermore, by separating the administration of Chaco War pensions from the other contributing plans and by requesting that the former be fully financed in the annual budget law, the reform will make explicit the cost to society of Chaco War pensions.

Besides legislative action, the government has started reorganizing the public pension administration and reviewing the rolls of beneficiaries. With assistance from the International Development Bank (IDB), the government recently hired an external consultant, PricewaterhouseCoopers, to help reorganize the pension administration and computerize its databases. On a separate but related front, the government is also completing a census of public employees that will eventually provide a detailed database of contributors to the pension system. In a second stage, the government plans to extend this census to the pension recipients, further deepening the cleanup of the registry of beneficiaries. These efforts to purge the registry of beneficiaries of fraudulent claims—which are believed to be widespread, especially in the administration of Chaco War pensions—should generate large savings.

## C. Assumptions and Methodology

To make projections about future contributions and pension disbursements, we need a variety of assumptions on demographic, macroeconomic, and sector-specific variables. This section describes our assumptions, together with the methodology that we use to calculate our actuarial projections. Tables 3.3 and 3.4 summarize the assumptions for the contributing plans and the Chaco War pensions, respectively.

### Demographics

Population projections for Paraguay are obtained from the World Development Indicators (WDI). The WDI provide projections for the future male and female population disaggregated by cohort; each cohort spans five years of age up to the cohort 70–74, except for the oldest cohort, which includes the population older than 75. Since projections are available only at a frequency of five years, we interpolate them to obtain projections for the intermediate years not covered by WDI.

These population projections allow us to compute the time evolution of the death rates by cohort that we employ in our study (Table 3.5). For example, because the cohort aged 25–29 in year 2025 turns into the cohort aged 30–34 in year 2030, we can compute the death rate for this cohort over the period 2025–30. As expected, the death rates decline over time across all the cohorts. However, the decline is more pronounced for the older cohorts, especially for the female population, as Paraguay's population ages.

### Table 3.3. Assumptions for Actuarial Computations on Contributing Plans

| | Public administration | | Army | |
|---|---|---|---|---|
| | *Before reform* | *After reform* | *Before reform* | *After reform* |
| Hiring policy | New hires maintain constant shares of active male and female public employees in total population. | Same number of new hires as before reform. | New hires maintain constant shares of active male and female officers in total population. | Same number of new hires as before reform. |
| Retirement age | Share of each cohort that is retired as in 2003. | Starting from 2004, no retirement before age 62; every employee retires at age 62. | Share of each cohort that is retired as in 2003. | Same as before reform. |
| Wage | Average wage of active employees. | Same as before reform. | Average wage of active officers. | Same as before reform. |
| Last wage | Estimated from average pension of retired employees using replacement rate of 93 percent. | Same as before reform. | Average pension of retired officers. | Same as before reform. |
| Wage growth | Nominal wage grows at inflation rate plus productivity growth rate. | Same as before reform. | Nominal wage grows at inflation rate plus productivity growth rate. | Same as before reform. |
| Contribution rate | 14 percent (on 13 monthly wages). | 16 percent (on 13 monthly wages). | 14 percent (on 13 monthly wages). | 16 percent (on 13 monthly wages). |
| Replacement rate | 93 percent. | 93 percent. | 100 percent. | 100 percent. |
| Aguinaldo | Paid. | Not paid. | Paid. | Not paid. |
| Base wage | Last wage. | Average of last wage in current and previous four years. | Last wage. | Average of last wage in current and previous four years. |
| Pension indexation | Growth rate of current nominal wage. | CPI inflation rate. | Growth rate of current nominal wage. | CPI inflation rate. |
| Number of survivor pensions | Constant share of survivor pensions to old-age pensions. | Same as before reform. | Constant share of survivor pensions to old-age pensions. | Same as before reform. |
| Amount of survivor pensions | Average survivor pension in 2003 adjusted by wage inflation (with aguinaldo). | Average survivor pension in 2003 adjusted by wage inflation (without aguinaldo). | Average survivor pension in 2003 adjusted by wage inflation (with aguinaldo). | Average survivor pension in 2003 adjusted by wage inflation (without aguinaldo). |

## Table 3.3 *(continued)*

| | Police | | Teachers | |
|---|---|---|---|---|
| | *Before reform* | *After reform* | *Before reform* | *After reform* |
| Hiring policy | New hires maintain constant shares of active male and female officers in total population. | Same number of new hires as before reform. | New hires maintain constant shares of active male and female teachers in population aged 5-19. | Same number of new hires as before reform. |
| Retirement age | Share of each cohort that is retired as in 2003. | Same as before reform. | Share of each cohort that is retired as in 2003. | Starting from 2004, no retirement before age 50; same as in 2003 for other cohorts. |
| Wage | Average wage of active officers. | Same as before reform. | Average wage of active teachers. | Same as before reform. |
| Last wage | Average pension of retired officers. | Same as before reform. | Estimated from average pension of retired officers using replacement rate of 93 percent. | Same as before reform. |
| Wage growth | Nominal wage grows at inflation rate plus productivity growth rate. | Same as before reform. | Nominal wage grows at inflation rate plus productivity growth rate. | Same as before reform. |
| Contribution rate | 14 percent (on 13 monthly wages). | 16 percent (on 13 monthly wages). | 14 percent (on 13 monthly wages). | 16 percent (on 13 monthly wages). |
| Replacement rate | 100 percent. | 100 percent. | 93 percent. | 87 percent. |
| Aguinaldo | Paid. | Not paid. | Paid. | Not paid. |
| Base wage | Last wage. | Average of last wage in current and previous four years. | Last wage. | Average of last wage in current and previous four years. |
| Pension indexation | Growth rate of current nominal wage. | CPI inflation rate. | Growth rate of current nominal wage. | CPI inflation rate. |
| Number of survivor pensions | Constant share of survivor pensions to old-age pensions. | Same as before reform. | Constant share of survivor pensions to old-age pensions. | Same as before reform. |
| Amount of survivor pensions | Average survivor pension in 2003 adjusted by wage inflation (with aguinaldo). | Average survivor pension in 2003 adjusted by wage inflation (without aguinaldo). | Average survivor pension in 2003 adjusted by wage inflation (with aguinaldo). | Average survivor pension in 2003 adjusted by wage inflation (without aguinaldo). |

**Table 3.3** *(concluded)*

| | University Professors | | Judicial Employees | |
|---|---|---|---|---|
| | *Before reform* | *After reform* | *Before reform* | *After reform* |
| Hiring policy | New hires maintain constant share of active male and female professors in total population. | Same number of new hires as before reform. | New hires maintain constant share of active male and female judges in total population. | Same number of new hires as before reform. |
| Retirement age | Share of each cohort that is retired as in 2003. | Starting from 2004, no retirement before age 62; same as in 2003 after age 62. Every professor retires after age 75. | Share of each cohort that is retired as in 2003. | Starting from 2004, no retirement before age 62; every employee retires after age 62. |
| Wage | Average wage of active professors. | Same as before reform. | Average wage of active judges. | Same as before reform. |
| Last wage | Estimated from average pension of retired employees using replacement rate of 93 percent. | Same as before reform. | Estimated from average pension of retired employees using replacement rate of 93 percent. | Same as before reform. |
| Wage growth | Nominal wage grows at inflation rate plus productivity growth rate. | Same as before reform. | Nominal wage grows at inflation rate plus productivity growth rate. | Same as before reform. |
| Contribution rate | 14 percent (on 13 monthly wages). | 16 percent (on 13 monthly wages). | 14 percent (on 13 monthly wages). | 16 percent (on 13 monthly wages). |
| Replacement rate | 93 percent. | 93 percent. | 93 percent. | 93 percent. |
| Aguinaldo | Paid. | Not paid. | Paid. | Not paid. |
| Base wage | Last wage. | Average of last wage in current and previous four years. | Last wage. | Average of last wage in current and previous four years. |
| Pension indexation | Growth rate of current nominal wage. | CPI inflation rate. | Growth rate of current nominal wage. | CPI inflation rate. |
| Number of survivor pensions | Constant share of survivor pensions to old-age pensions. | Same as before reform. | Constant share of survivor pensions to old-age pensions. | Same as before reform. |
| Amount of survivor pensions | Average survivor pension in 2003 adjusted by wage inflation (with aguinaldo). | Average survivor pension in 2003 adjusted by wage inflation (without aguinaldo). | Average survivor pension in 2003 adjusted by wage inflation (with aguinaldo). | Average survivor pension in 2003 adjusted by wage inflation (without aguinaldo). |

Sources: Ministry of finance; and Fund staff analyses.

**Table 3.4.  Assumptions for Actuarial Computations on Chaco War Pensions**

|  | Before Reform | After Reform |
|---|---|---|
| Creation of new survivor pensions | In case of death of a veteran, a new pension is paid to a female survivor aged 50–54. | Same as before reform. |
| Elimination of veteran pensions | In case of death only. | Same as before reform. |
| Elimination of survivor pensions | In case of death only (also for pensions of single daughters). | Same as before reform. |
| Replacement rate for survivor pensions | 100 percent of veteran pension. | 75 percent of veteran pension. |
| Aguinaldo | Paid. | Not paid. |
| Pension indexation | Growth rate of current nominal wage. | CPI inflation rate. |

Sources: Ministry of Finance; and Fund staff analyses.

The Ministry of Finance provided us with data on active public employees as of October 2003. These data included, for each category of public employees covered by the caja fiscal, information on monthly wages and contributions by age and gender. Unfortunately, the information on age turned out to be very inaccurate since, for a large number of employees, age was either missing or implausible. As a result, we had to discard those individuals for whom age was either missing or implausible to estimate the age distribution of the active employees in 2003. Subsequently, we allocated the individuals with missing or inaccurate age information to the various cohorts using the estimated age distribution.[65] For each category of public employees, we computed annual wages and contributions in 2003 by multiplying the monthly contributions by 13 (since contributions are paid on the aguinaldo as well).

The Ministry of Finance also provided us with data on pension recipients as of October 2003. The data consisted of all the individual records of pension recipients in the caja fiscal. A complete record includes gender, type of pension (i.e., ordinary or early retirement), age at retirement, current age, and monthly pension but, unfortunately, no information on the length of service at the time of retirement. As for the age information on active employees, we found many gaps in the individual records. As for the active employees, therefore, we first had to compute the age distribution of current pension recipients on the subsample of recipients for whom age information was available and then use the resulting

---

[65]In other words, we implicitly assumed that the inaccuracy in age information was random.

### Table 3.5. Death Rates by Cohort[1]
*(In percent)*

|  | 2005 | 2010 | 2020 | 2030 | 2040 | 2050 |
|---|---|---|---|---|---|---|
| **Males** | | | | | | |
| 20–24 | –0.1 | –0.2 | –0.1 | –0.1 | –0.1 | –0.1 |
| 25–29 | –0.2 | –0.1 | –0.1 | –0.1 | –0.1 | –0.1 |
| 30–34 | –0.2 | –0.2 | –0.1 | –0.1 | –0.1 | –0.1 |
| 35–39 | –0.2 | –0.2 | –0.1 | –0.2 | –0.1 | –0.1 |
| 40–44 | –0.2 | –0.2 | –0.3 | –0.2 | –0.2 | –0.1 |
| 45–49 | –0.4 | –0.5 | –0.4 | –0.3 | –0.3 | –0.3 |
| 50–54 | –0.8 | –0.7 | –0.7 | –0.5 | –0.5 | –0.4 |
| 55–59 | –1.1 | –1.0 | –1.0 | –0.9 | –0.9 | –0.7 |
| 60–64 | –2.0 | –2.0 | –1.6 | –1.4 | –1.3 | –1.2 |
| 65–69 | –3.0 | –2.6 | –2.4 | –2.2 | –1.9 | –1.7 |
| 70–74 | –4.2 | –4.1 | –3.7 | –3.4 | –3.0 | –2.6 |
| 75+ | –18.3 | –15.9 | –16.1 | –16.0 | –13.3 | –12.9 |
| **Females** | | | | | | |
| 20–24 | –0.1 | –0.1 | –0.1 | –0.1 | –0.1 | –0.1 |
| 25–29 | –0.1 | –0.1 | –0.1 | 0.0 | –0.1 | 0.0 |
| 30–34 | –0.1 | –0.1 | –0.1 | –0.1 | –0.1 | –0.1 |
| 35–39 | –0.1 | –0.1 | –0.1 | –0.1 | 0.0 | –0.1 |
| 40–44 | –0.1 | –0.2 | –0.2 | –0.1 | –0.1 | –0.1 |
| 45–49 | –0.3 | –0.4 | –0.2 | –0.2 | –0.2 | –0.1 |
| 50–54 | –0.5 | –0.4 | –0.3 | –0.4 | –0.3 | –0.2 |
| 55–59 | –0.5 | –0.5 | –0.5 | –0.5 | –0.4 | –0.4 |
| 60–64 | –1.0 | –1.1 | –0.9 | –0.7 | –0.6 | –0.5 |
| 65–69 | –2.0 | –1.7 | –1.3 | –1.2 | –1.0 | –0.8 |
| 70–74 | –3.2 | –2.7 | –2.6 | –2.1 | –1.7 | –1.5 |
| 75+ | –15.9 | –15.2 | –12.9 | –12.7 | –10.4 | –9.7 |

Sources: World Development Indicators; and Fund staff estimates.

[1]The minus sign denotes a positive death rate.

distribution to allocate the individuals with missing or inaccurate age information to the various cohorts.[66] For each category of pension recipients, we computed annual pension disbursements in 2003 by multiplying the monthly disbursements by 13 (to account for the payment of aguinaldo).

### Retirement decisions

Future pension disbursements depend on future retirement decisions, which in turn depend on the incentives and requirements contained in the pension law.

---

[66]It is worth noting that our implicit assumption that information inaccuracy is random may be particularly delicate in this context, as missing information may conceal fraud and thus be nonrandom.

Modeling retirement decisions is therefore critical for the evolution of pension disbursements. To model these decisions, we made the following assumptions:

- The individual attitudes toward retirement can be described entirely by the share of each cohort of the total population of active and retired employees who, at each point in time, are retired. For example, if, in 2003, a share of 20 percent of all the active and retired teachers aged 50–54 are retired, this means that individual preferences toward work and retirement are such that 20 percent of the teachers of this age choose to retire, given their years of service, the minimum service requirements, the replacement rates, and the other provisions in the pension law. Table 3.6 shows the share of pension recipients by cohort across the various pension plans in 2003 before the reform.

- The individual attitudes toward retirement remain constant over time. That is, holding the pension law and future wages unchanged, the same share of each cohort of the total population of active and retired employees is retired during each year.

- Given the previous two assumptions, we computed the number of employees who retire every year to keep the shares of pension recipients within each cohort constant over time.

- The new law affects the shares of employees who retire during each year if it raises the minimum retirement age or introduces mandatory retirement. Accordingly, we adjust the share of employees who retire within each cohort if the pension reform affects the retirement age. For example, if retirement becomes mandatory at 62, as is the case for public administration employees, then 60 percent of the cohort aged 60–64 (corresponding to the individuals who are 62 or older in this cohort) and 100 percent of the older cohorts retire after the reform; for all the younger cohorts, this share is zero. On the other hand, if a cohort is not affected by the increase in the retirement age, as is the case for army and police officers, then the same share of employees retire before and after the reform—that is, we ignore the effect that other changes introduced by the reform (such as in the replacement rates) may have on retirement decisions. Table 3.6 summarizes the effect of the reform on the shares of retired employees for all the contributing plans.

- Data limitations prevent us from considering the years of service as a determinant of retirement.

### Table 3.6. Assumptions on Retirement Age by Cohort and Pension Plan
*(Percent of retirees per cohort)*

| | Public Administration | | Army | | Police | |
|---|---|---|---|---|---|---|
| | Before reform | After reform | Before reform | After reform | Before reform | After reform |
| **Males** | | | | | | |
| 30–34 | 0.0 | 0.0 | 0.6 | 0.6 | 0.0 | 0.0 |
| 35–39 | 0.3 | 0.0 | 1.3 | 1.3 | 0.7 | 0.7 |
| 40–44 | 1.0 | 0.0 | 4.8 | 4.8 | 2.8 | 2.8 |
| 45–49 | 4.0 | 0.0 | 11.9 | 11.9 | 6.5 | 6.5 |
| 50–54 | 10.5 | 0.0 | 34.5 | 34.5 | 24.5 | 24.5 |
| 55–59 | 24.7 | 0.0 | 67.6 | 67.6 | 49.7 | 49.7 |
| 60–64 | 42.4 | 60.0 | 80.2 | 80.2 | 73.6 | 73.6 |
| 65–69 | 60.6 | 100.0 | 84.2 | 84.2 | 96.0 | 96.0 |
| 70–74 | 70.6 | 100.0 | 87.0 | 87.0 | 97.8 | 97.8 |
| 75+ | 81.3 | 100.0 | 92.1 | 92.1 | 97.6 | 97.6 |
| **Females** | | | | | | |
| 30–34 | 0.0 | 0.0 | 0.0 | 0.0 | 0.4 | 0.4 |
| 35–39 | 0.2 | 0.0 | 0.4 | 0.4 | 1.2 | 1.2 |
| 40–44 | 1.3 | 0.0 | 0.0 | 0.0 | 3.2 | 3.2 |
| 45–49 | 5.9 | 0.0 | 0.8 | 0.8 | 4.8 | 4.8 |
| 50–54 | 16.0 | 0.0 | 5.5 | 5.5 | 11.9 | 11.9 |
| 55–59 | 34.3 | 0.0 | 26.2 | 26.2 | 23.5 | 23.5 |
| 60–64 | 52.9 | 60.0 | 47.1 | 47.1 | 48.8 | 48.8 |
| 65–69 | 70.3 | 100.0 | 48.6 | 48.6 | 80.7 | 80.7 |
| 70–74 | 78.9 | 100.0 | 64.9 | 64.9 | 100.0 | 100.0 |
| 75+ | 89.4 | 100.0 | 83.0 | 83.0 | 100.0 | 100.0 |

| | Teachers | | University Professors | | Judicial Employees | |
|---|---|---|---|---|---|---|
| | Before reform | After reform | Before reform | After reform | Before reform | After reform |
| **Males** | | | | | | |
| 30–34 | 0.0 | 0.0 | 0.0 | 0.0 | 0.0 | 0.0 |
| 35–39 | 0.0 | 0.0 | 0.0 | 0.0 | 0.0 | 0.0 |
| 40–44 | 0.1 | 0.0 | 0.0 | 0.0 | 0.0 | 0.0 |
| 45–49 | 2.9 | 0.0 | 1.2 | 0.0 | 0.5 | 0.0 |
| 50–54 | 20.0 | 20.0 | 3.3 | 0.0 | 10.9 | 0.0 |
| 55–59 | 33.4 | 33.4 | 6.9 | 0.0 | 20.9 | 0.0 |
| 60–64 | 47.0 | 47.0 | 18.6 | 11.2 | 47.6 | 60.0 |
| 65–69 | 47.0 | 47.0 | 29.1 | 29.1 | 54.4 | 100.0 |
| 70–74 | 52.8 | 52.8 | 34.0 | 34.0 | 67.9 | 100.0 |
| 75+ | 100.0 | 100.0 | 60.2 | 100.0 | 96.3 | 100.0 |
| **Females** | | | | | | |
| 30–34 | 0.0 | 0.0 | 0.0 | 0.0 | 0.0 | 0.0 |
| 35–39 | 0.0 | 0.0 | 0.0 | 0.0 | 0.0 | 0.0 |
| 40–44 | 1.5 | 0.0 | 0.0 | 0.0 | 0.0 | 0.0 |
| 45–49 | 15.6 | 0.0 | 3.5 | 0.0 | 1.7 | 0.0 |
| 50–54 | 46.6 | 46.6 | 8.4 | 0.0 | 4.4 | 0.0 |
| 55–59 | 70.4 | 70.4 | 10.5 | 0.0 | 25.6 | 0.0 |
| 60–64 | 84.1 | 84.1 | 13.1 | 7.8 | 31.9 | 60.0 |
| 65–69 | 89.2 | 89.2 | 16.4 | 16.4 | 19.4 | 100.0 |
| 70–74 | 90.4 | 90.4 | 30.8 | 30.8 | 59.0 | 100.0 |
| 75+ | 100.0 | 100.0 | 55.8 | 100.0 | 100.0 | 100.0 |

Sources: Ministry of Finance; and Fund staff estimates.

## Contributions

Future contributions depend on the future evolution of the population of active employees. Determining the evolution of the active population is particularly difficult in the present context, since it depends not only on the future demographic developments at the country level but also on the government's future policies regarding the size of the public sector. In this study, we sought to keep a neutral stance by making the following assumptions:

- As regards teachers, in the prereform scenario, every year the government hires new male and female 24-year-old teachers to keep the ratios of active male and female teachers to the population aged 5–19 constant at the 2003 level.

- As regards the other plans, in the prereform scenario, every year the government hires new male and female 24-year-old employees to keep the ratios of active male and female employees to the whole population constant at the 2003 level.[67]

- The same number of new employees is hired every year under the postreform scenario as in the prereform scenario. This assumption implies that although the total population of active and retired employees is equal in the pre- and postreform scenarios, its composition in terms of active and retired employees is different (if retirement decisions are different).

- Finally, the population of active employees declines only as a result of death or retirement of active employees.

We computed the contributions to each pension plan during a given year by multiplying the number of active employees, the average annual wage, and the contribution rate. The contribution rate is 14 percent before the reform and 16 percent after the reform. The evolution of future wages is described below.

## Old-age pensions

Future wages matter for future contributions and for the future pensions of newly retired employees. In particular, an employee's wage history at the time of retirement determines the base wage, which is used in turn to compute the initial

---

[67]To better match the data, new male hires for the army are 19 years old.

pension. To compute the evolution of average wages and wage histories, we made the following simplifying assumptions:

- For each category of workers, we computed a measure of the last (nominal) wage of a newly retired employee in 2003 as the average of the pensions paid in 2003, adjusted for the relevant replacement rate. Two features of the prereform pension plans—that the base wage coincides with the last wage and that old pensions are indexed to the current wage growth—imply that this yields an accurate yet straightforward measure of the last wage of new pension-recipient employees in 2003.

- We assumed that average and last wages grow at an annual rate equal to the sum of CPI inflation and productivity growth. The latter is defined as the difference between real GDP growth and population growth. This assumption implies that we keep the slope of the wage structure constant over the horizon of our study.

The base wage is a key variable for the evolution of pension disbursements. Together with the replacement rates, it determines the initial pension for new pension recipients. In the prereform scenario, we compute the base wage as the last wage; in the postreform scenario, we compute it as the average of the last nominal wages in the current and the previous four years.[68] It is worth noting that the new law does not require that past wages be adjusted for inflation when computing the base wage, although old pensions are indexed to CPI inflation.

The new law modifies the replacement rates. In our study, we accommodated for these changes as follows:

- As regards teachers, we used a replacement rate of 87 percent in the postreform scenario, down from 93 percent in the prereform scenario—we thus ignored the possibility that teachers can retire early at the replacement rate of 83 percent.

- As regards public administration employees, university professors, and judicial employees, the new law makes the replacement rate dependent on the years of service at the time of retirement. Since we lacked information on years of service, we used the same replacement rate of 93 percent in the pre- and postreform scenarios.

---

[68]As a conservative assumption, we do not allow for the lengthening to 10 years of the period used to compute the base wage for teachers. The new law allows for this lengthening if a teacher works considerably more hours or shifts at the end of his or her career.

- As regards army and police officers, the new law does not change the replacement rates (which vary as a function of years of service). Since the replacement rate can rise to 100 percent (after 30 years of service), we assumed conservatively the highest replacement rate of 100 percent in the pre- and postreform scenarios.

We computed the annual pension disbursements for each pension plan as the sum of new pensions and the pensions of the pensioners surviving from the previous year. This required the following steps:

- We computed the total amount of new pensions by multiplying the number of new pension recipients, the monthly amount of a new pension, and the number of months a pension is paid during the year.

- We computed the total amount of old pensions by multiplying the number of existing pensioners who survive (using the cohort-specific death rates in Table 3.5), the adjusted monthly pension from the previous year, and the number of months a pension is paid.

- We adjusted the nominal value of pensions by the growth rate of wages for active employees in the prereform scenario and by CPI inflation in the postreform scenario.

## Survivor and Chaco War pensions

Data limitations prevented us from modeling the evolution of survivor pensions in detail. Thus, we made the following simplifying assumptions:

- The ratio of survivor pensions to old-age pensions remains constant over time at its value in 2003.

- Nominal survivor pensions grow at the same rate as old-age pensions.

There are two categories of Chaco War pensions, those paid to the war veterans themselves and those paid to their survivors. As for the data on active employees and old-age pension recipients, the data exhibited many gaps that forced us to estimate the age distributions of the various categories on subsamples of the population of pensioners. To model the evolution over time of these two categories of pensions, we made the following assumptions:

- We assumed that the number of veteran pensions declines only as a result of death. Therefore, in our calculations we ignored the effect that the ongoing efforts to purge the registry of beneficiaries may have on the number of pensions.

- We assumed that, when a veteran dies, a new survivor pension is created; in particular, the survivor is female, aged 50–54.

- We assumed that the number of survivor pensions declines only as a result of death. As for the veteran pensions, we ignored the effect of purging the registry of beneficiaries.

- We assumed a replacement rate for new survivor pensions of 100 in the prereform scenario and 75 percent in the postreform scenario.

- We assumed that pensions are indexed to the growth of nominal wages for public administration employees in the prereform scenario and to CPI inflation in the postadministration scenario.

## Thirteen-month bonus (*aguinaldo*)

Aguinaldo to recipients of old-age, survivor, and Chaco War pensions is paid in the prereform scenario but not in the postreform scenario. This implies that the monthly pension is paid 13 times in the prereform scenario and 12 times in the postreform scenario.

## Macroeconomic assumptions

Finally, we needed a few macroeconomic assumptions. These are summarized in Table 3.7 for selected years. In the long run, real GDP is assumed to grow at an annual rate of 3.4 percent, and inflation is assumed to be stable at 6 percent. The real interest rate is assumed constant at 5 percent; the assumption on the real interest rate is critical for determining the net present value of deficits of a pension plan but does not affect the size of the operational deficits. Finally, we computed productivity growth as the difference between GDP growth and population growth.

### Table 3.7. Paraguay: Macroeconomic Assumptions

|  | 2004 | 2005 | 2010 | 2020 | 2030 | 2040 | 2050 |
|---|---|---|---|---|---|---|---|
| GDP at constant prices (percent change) | 2.7 | 3.2 | 3.4 | 3.4 | 3.4 | 3.4 | 3.4 |
| CPI inflation | 8.0 | 6.0 | 6.0 | 6.0 | 6.0 | 6.0 | 6.0 |
| Real interest rate (percent) | 5.0 | 5.0 | 5.0 | 5.0 | 5.0 | 5.0 | 5.0 |
| Productivity growth[1] | 0.3 | 0.8 | 1.4 | 2.0 | 2.2 | 2.4 | 2.7 |

Source: Central Bank of Paraguay; and Fund staff estimates.

[1]Difference between GDP growth and population growth.

83

## D. Findings

### Prereform scenario

In the prereform scenario, the balance between active workers and pension recipients worsens dramatically over 2003–50 (Figure 3.1). For the contributing plans as a whole, the dependency ratio more than doubles over this period, rising from 0.22 to 0.55. The increase in this ratio affects all the contributing plans, but it is particularly steep for the largest plan (for teachers), where the ratio quadruples to 0.8 between 2003 and 2050. With regard to Chaco War pensions, although the number of veteran pensions quickly dwindles to zero as old veterans die, the number of survivor pensions falls more gradually, an implication of the relatively young age of current survivors and of our conservative assumption that a female survivor aged 50–54 replaces each dying veteran.

Worsening dependency ratios generate rapidly growing operational deficits (Table 3.8. In the prereform scenario, the caja fiscal is on an explosive path, with the net present value of deficits in 2003–50 approaching 90 percent of initial GDP,[69] as the operational deficit in percent of GDP grows from 1.5 percent to 4.2 percent in 2050. The contributing plans account for almost all of these cumulated deficits (about 78 percent of initial GDP), with the Chaco War pensions accounting for the rest (just below 7 percent of initial GDP).

Three plans—for teachers, the army, and the police—account for more than three-fourths of the net present value of deficits of the contributing plans. In the prereform scenario, the plan for teachers, in particular, generates a net present value of deficits of almost 35 percent of initial GDP, as its operational deficit in percent of GDP grows from 0.2 percent in 2003 to 1.7 percent in 2050, boosted by a threefold increase in disbursements not matched by an increase in contributions—contributions as a percent of GDP remain more or less flat over the period under consideration.[70] The pension plans for the army and the police also experience steep increases in their operational deficits—their joint deficit climbs to almost 1 percent of GDP in 2050—generating net present values of deficits of about 18 and 15 percent of initial GDP, respectively.

---

[69]Box 3.1 explains the details behind the computation of net present values in percent of initial GDP.

[70]Contributions from active teachers decline starting in 2020 as the number of active teachers declines. This decline, in turn, is an implication of our assumptions that the number of active teachers in proportion to the population aged 5–19 remains constant over time. As the latter is expected to undergo a temporary decline starting in 2020, contributions from active teachers decline with the decline in the population of active teachers.

## Figure 3.1. Demographic Evolutions of Pension Plans in the Prereform Scenario

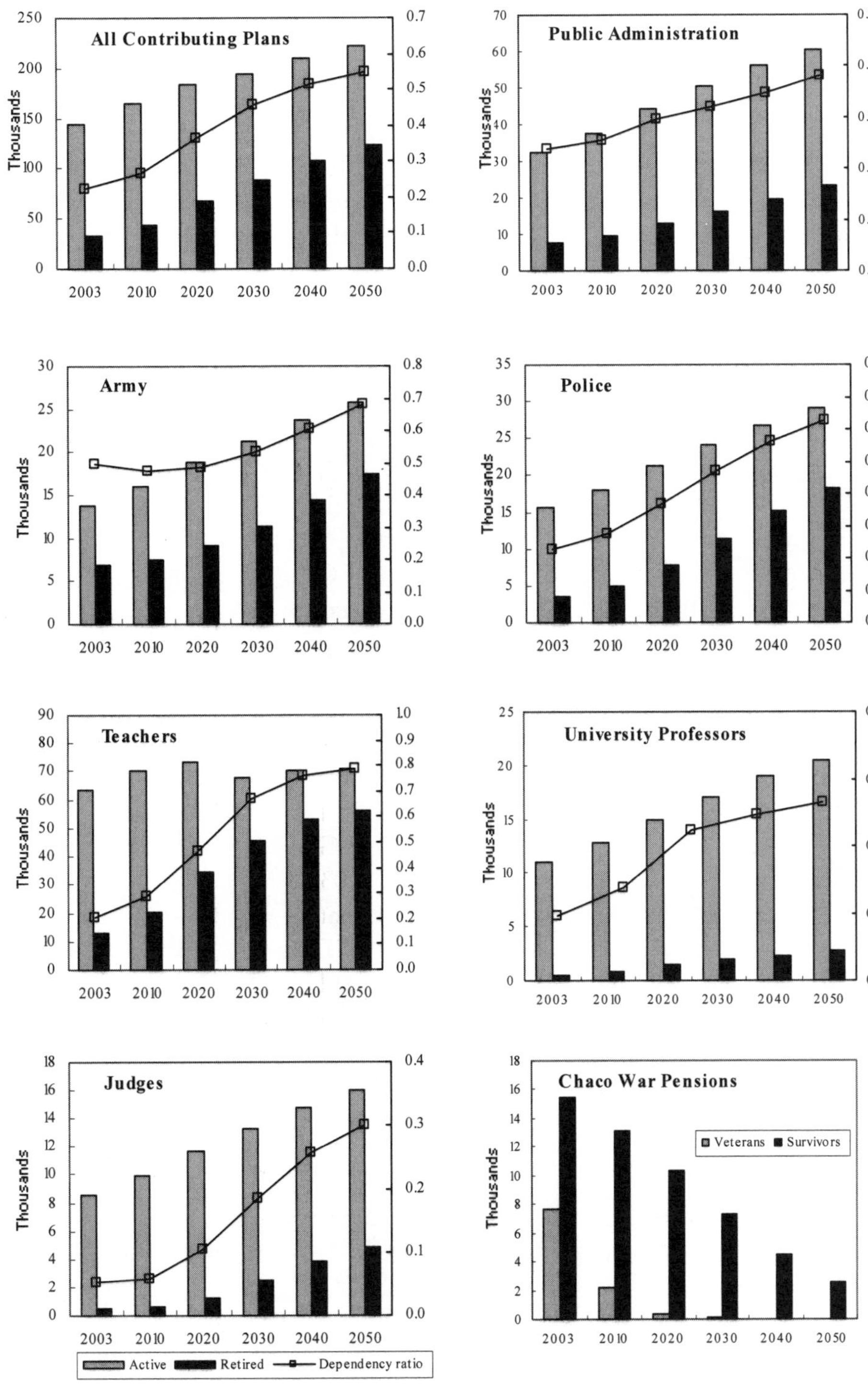

Sources: Ministry of Finance; and Fund staff estimates.

### Table 3.8. Actuarial Balances in the Prereform Scenario
*(Percent of GDP)*

| | 2003 | 2004 | 2005 | 2010 | 2020 | 2030 | 2040 | 2050 | NPV[1] |
|---|---|---|---|---|---|---|---|---|---|
| Caja Fiscal | −1.5 | −1.5 | −1.4 | −1.6 | −2.3 | −3 | −3.7 | −4.2 | −86.5 |
| Contributions | 0.9 | 1.0 | 1.0 | 1.0 | 1.0 | 1.0 | 1.1 | 1.1 | 34.8 |
| Disbursements | 2.4 | 2.4 | 2.4 | 2.6 | 3.3 | 4.0 | 4.7 | 5.4 | 121.4 |
| | | | | | | | | | |
| Contributing plans[2] | −0.8 | −0.9 | −0.9 | −1.2 | −2 | −2.9 | −3.6 | −4.2 | −77.8 |
| Contributions | 0.9 | 1.0 | 1.0 | 1.0 | 1.0 | 1.0 | 1.1 | 1.1 | 34.8 |
| Disbursements | 1.8 | 1.8 | 1.8 | 2.2 | 3.0 | 3.9 | 4.6 | 5.3 | 112.7 |
| | | | | | | | | | |
| Public administration | −0.1 | −0.1 | −0.1 | −0.1 | −0.2 | −0.3 | −0.3 | −0.4 | −8.1 |
| Contributions | 0.2 | 0.2 | 0.2 | 0.2 | 0.2 | 0.2 | 0.3 | 0.3 | 7.5 |
| Disbursements | 0.3 | 0.3 | 0.3 | 0.3 | 0.4 | 0.5 | 0.6 | 0.7 | 15.6 |
| | | | | | | | | | |
| Army | −0.4 | −0.4 | −0.4 | −0.4 | −0.5 | −0.6 | −0.7 | −0.9 | −18.1 |
| Contributions | 0.1 | 0.1 | 0.1 | 0.1 | 0.1 | 0.1 | 0.1 | 0.1 | 3.4 |
| Disbursements | 0.5 | 0.5 | 0.5 | 0.5 | 0.6 | 0.7 | 0.8 | 1.0 | 21.5 |
| | | | | | | | | | |
| Police | −0.2 | −0.2 | −0.2 | −0.2 | −0.4 | −0.6 | −0.7 | −0.9 | −15.5 |
| Contributions | 0.1 | 0.1 | 0.1 | 0.1 | 0.1 | 0.1 | 0.1 | 0.1 | 3.9 |
| Disbursements | 0.3 | 0.3 | 0.3 | 0.3 | 0.5 | 0.7 | 0.9 | 1.1 | 19.4 |
| | | | | | | | | | |
| University professors | 0.0 | 0.0 | 0.0 | 0.0 | 0.0 | −0.1 | −0.1 | −0.1 | −1.3 |
| Contributions | 0.0 | 0.0 | 0.0 | 0.1 | 0.1 | 0.1 | 0.1 | 0.1 | 2.0 |
| Disbursements | 0.0 | 0.0 | 0.0 | 0.1 | 0.1 | 0.1 | 0.1 | 0.2 | 3.3 |
| | | | | | | | | | |
| Judicial employees | 0.1 | 0.1 | 0.1 | 0.1 | 0.0 | 0.0 | −0.1 | −0.1 | −0.2 |
| Contributions | 0.1 | 0.1 | 0.1 | 0.1 | 0.1 | 0.1 | 0.1 | 0.1 | 3.3 |
| Disbursements | 0.0 | 0.0 | 0.0 | 0.0 | 0.1 | 0.1 | 0.2 | 0.2 | 3.5 |
| | | | | | | | | | |
| Teachers | −0.2 | −0.2 | −0.3 | −0.5 | −1 | −1.4 | −1.6 | −1.7 | −34.7 |
| Contributions | 0.5 | 0.5 | 0.5 | 0.5 | 0.4 | 0.4 | 0.4 | 0.4 | 14.7 |
| Disbursements | 0.7 | 0.7 | 0.7 | 0.9 | 1.4 | 1.8 | 2.0 | 2.2 | 49.4 |
| | | | | | | | | | |
| Chaco War pensions | −0.7 | −0.6 | −0.6 | −0.4 | −0.2 | −0.2 | −0.1 | −0.1 | −8.7 |
| Veterans | 0.3 | 0.2 | 0.2 | 0.1 | 0.0 | 0.0 | 0.0 | 0.0 | 1.4 |
| Survivors | 0.4 | 0.4 | 0.4 | 0.3 | 0.2 | 0.2 | 0.1 | 0.1 | 7.3 |

Sources: Ministry of Finance; and Fund staff estimates.

[1]NPV represents net present values of balances, contributions, and disbursements between 2003 and 2050 at an annual real interest rate of 5 percent.

[2]Disbursements for contributing plans include old–age and survivors pensions.

---

### Box 3.1. Computing Net Present Values of Future Deficits

In this study, we use net present value calculations extensively. This box presents the analytical underpinnings for such calculations, following Chand and Jaeger (1996).

Let $b_t$, $d_t$, $r_t$, and $g_t$ denote the debt position accumulated at the beginning of year $t$ in percent of GDP in year $t$, the operational deficit of a given pension plan in year $t$ (defined as the difference between disbursements and contributions) in percent of GDP in year $t$, the real interest rate in year $t$, and the growth rate of real GDP in year $t$. Then, the debt position of the pension plan evolves as

$$b_{t+1} = R_t b_t + d_t,$$

where the capitalization factor $R_t$ is defined as $R_t \equiv (1 + r_t)/(1 + g_t)$. This equation implies that the debt position in percent of GDP at the beginning of year $t+N$ is equal to

$$b_{t+N} = \left( \prod_{j=0}^{N-1} R_{t+j} \right) b_t + \sum_{j=0}^{N-1} \left( \prod_{k=j}^{N-1} d_{t+k} \right).$$

From this equation, the net present value of the deficits incurred in year $t$ through year $t+N-1$ (in percent of GDP in the initial year $t$) is given by

$$\tilde{b}_{t+N} = \frac{b_{t+N}}{\left( \prod_{j=0}^{N-1} R_{t+j} \right)}.$$

If the initial debt position is zero, $b_t = 0$, then $\tilde{b}_{t+N}$ coincides with the net present values of future deficits using (approximately) the interest rates $r_t - g_t$, $r_{t+1} - g_{t+1}$, etc., that is, the difference between the real interest rates and the rates of growth of GDP; this is the notion of net present value that we use in the main text. If the initial debt position were different from zero, then it would have to be added to the net present value of future deficits.

Despite the old age of veterans, Chaco War pensions generate deficits with a net present value of almost 9 percent of initial GDP. Offsetting the rapid decline in the number of veteran pensions, survivor pensions continue to generate sizable operational deficits well into the future. This behavior reflects the slow decline in the number of survivor pensions that was pointed out earlier (Figure 3.1).

### Postreform scenario

The reform generates major savings but does not achieve financial balance over time (Table 3.9). The reform tackles the prereform explosive dynamics by cutting the net present value of deficits by more than half. However, it leaves large

### Table 3.9.  Actuarial Balances in the Postreform Scenario
*(Percent of GDP)*

|  | 2003 | 2004 | 2005 | 2010 | 2020 | 2030 | 2040 | 2050 | NPV[1] |
|---|---|---|---|---|---|---|---|---|---|
| Caja Fiscal | −1.5 | −1.0 | −1.0 | −0.9 | −1.2 | −1.5 | −1.8 | −1.9 | −45.0 |
| Contributions | 0.9 | 1.1 | 1.1 | 1.1 | 1.2 | 1.2 | 1.2 | 1.3 | 39.9 |
| Disbursements | 2.4 | 2.1 | 2.1 | 2.0 | 2.3 | 2.7 | 3.0 | 3.2 | 84.9 |
| Contributing plans[2] | −0.8 | −0.5 | −0.5 | −0.6 | −1.0 | −1.4 | −1.7 | −1.9 | −38.2 |
| Contributions | 0.9 | 1.1 | 1.1 | 1.1 | 1.2 | 1.2 | 1.2 | 1.3 | 39.9 |
| Disbursements | 1.8 | 1.6 | 1.6 | 1.7 | 2.2 | 2.6 | 2.9 | 3.2 | 78.1 |
| Public administration | −0.1 | −0.1 | −0.1 | −0.1 | −0.1 | −0.1 | −0.1 | −0.2 | −3.2 |
| Contributions | 0.2 | 0.2 | 0.2 | 0.2 | 0.2 | 0.3 | 0.3 | 0.3 | 8.5 |
| Disbursements | 0.3 | 0.3 | 0.3 | 0.3 | 0.3 | 0.4 | 0.4 | 0.5 | 11.7 |
| Army | −0.4 | −0.3 | −0.3 | −0.3 | −0.3 | −0.4 | −0.4 | −0.5 | −12.7 |
| Contributions | 0.1 | 0.1 | 0.1 | 0.1 | 0.1 | 0.1 | 0.1 | 0.1 | 3.8 |
| Disbursements | 0.5 | 0.4 | 0.4 | 0.4 | 0.4 | 0.5 | 0.6 | 0.7 | 16.5 |
| Police | −0.2 | −0.1 | −0.1 | −0.2 | −0.2 | −0.3 | −0.4 | −0.5 | −9.7 |
| Contributions | 0.1 | 0.1 | 0.1 | 0.1 | 0.1 | 0.1 | 0.2 | 0.2 | 4.5 |
| Disbursements | 0.3 | 0.2 | 0.2 | 0.3 | 0.4 | 0.5 | 0.6 | 0.7 | 14.1 |
| University professors | 0.0 | 0.0 | 0.0 | 0.0 | 0.0 | 0.0 | 0.0 | 0.0 | −0.1 |
| Contributions | 0.0 | 0.1 | 0.1 | 0.1 | 0.1 | 0.1 | 0.1 | 0.1 | 2.3 |
| Disbursements | 0.0 | 0.0 | 0.0 | 0.0 | 0.1 | 0.1 | 0.1 | 0.1 | 2.4 |
| Judicial employees | 0.1 | 0.1 | 0.1 | 0.1 | 0.1 | 0.0 | 0.0 | −0.1 | 0.7 |
| Contributions | 0.1 | 0.1 | 0.1 | 0.1 | 0.1 | 0.1 | 0.1 | 0.1 | 3.7 |
| Disbursements | 0.0 | 0.0 | 0.0 | 0.0 | 0.1 | 0.1 | 0.2 | 0.2 | 3.0 |
| Teachers | −0.2 | 0.0 | 0.0 | −0.1 | −0.4 | −0.6 | −0.6 | −0.6 | −13.2 |
| Contributions | 0.5 | 0.5 | 0.5 | 0.5 | 0.5 | 0.5 | 0.5 | 0.5 | 17.1 |
| Disbursements | 0.7 | 0.6 | 0.6 | 0.7 | 0.9 | 1.1 | 1.1 | 1.1 | 30.4 |
| Chaco War pensions | −0.7 | −0.6 | −0.5 | −0.3 | −0.2 | −0.1 | 0.0 | 0.0 | −6.7 |
| Veterans | 0.3 | 0.2 | 0.2 | 0.1 | 0.0 | 0.0 | 0.0 | 0.0 | 1.2 |
| Survivors | 0.4 | 0.4 | 0.3 | 0.3 | 0.2 | 0.1 | 0.0 | 0.0 | 5.5 |

Sources: Ministry of Finance; and Fund staff estimates.

[1]NPV represents net present values of balances, contributions, and disbursements between 2003 and 2050 at an annual real interest rate of 5 percent.
[2]Disbursements for contributing plans include old-age and survivors pensions.

unfunded liabilities, in the form of a net present value of deficits of about 45 percent of initial GDP for the caja fiscal (38 percent of GDP for the contributing plans as a whole). The pension plans for teachers and army officers continue to be the plans generating the highest net present value of deficits between 2003 and 2050 (about 13 percent of initial GDP each).

Although the reform generates savings across the board, the financial situation of some plans continues to cause concern. With regard to the impact on the components of the caja fiscal, the following facts deserve consideration:

- The reform generates savings worth, in net present value terms, about 20 percent of initial GDP for the teachers' plan. However, this plan, which accounts for almost half of the prereform net present value of deficits, continues to generate a net present value of deficits of more than 13 percent of initial GDP.

- The reform has a relatively small impact on the plans for police and army officers. The reform reduces the combined net present value of their deficits by about one-third, from more than 30 percent of initial GDP in the prereform scenario to about 20 percent of initial GDP in the postreform scenario.

- The reform brings the plans for judicial employees and university professors into financial balance. However, these plans are too small to generate a large impact on the overall deficit of the caja fiscal.

- The reform almost achieves long-term equilibrium in the plan for public administration employees, bringing the net present value of deficits to 3 percent of initial GDP.

- As regards Chaco War pensions, the reform generates savings of 0.1 percent of GDP in 2004 and of about 2 percent of initial GDP in net present value terms. These savings accrue almost entirely from lowering survivor pensions.

The relative importance of the sources of savings changes over time (Table 3.10). We can summarize our main findings about the sources of savings from reforming the contributing plans as follows:[71]

---

[71]Box 3.2 explains our method of identifying the sources of savings.

#### Table 3.10.  Estimated Savings from Reforming the Contributing Plans [1]

| | 2003 | 2004 | 2005 | 2010 | 2020 | 2030 | 2040 | 2050 | NPV[2] |
|---|---|---|---|---|---|---|---|---|---|
| Overall balance | | | | Percent of GDP | | | | | |
| Before reform | –0.8 | –0.9 | –0.9 | –1.2 | –2.0 | –2.9 | –3.6 | –4.2 | –77.8 |
| After reform | –0.8 | –0.5 | –0.5 | –0.6 | –1.0 | –1.4 | –1.7 | –1.9 | –38.2 |
| Savings | – | 0.4 | 0.4 | 0.6 | 1.0 | 1.4 | 1.8 | 2.3 | 39.6 |
| Source of savings: | | | | Percent of Savings | | | | | |
| Raising retirement age[3] | – | 17.7 | 18.0 | 15.4 | 5.6 | 0.1 | –2.4 | –3.1 | 2.4 |
| Lowering pension benefits | – | 6.5 | 12.9 | 35.9 | 61.8 | 74.7 | 81.3 | 84.7 | 69.0 |
| Abolishing aguinaldo | – | 30.9 | 27.8 | 19.8 | 14.9 | 12.7 | 11.0 | 9.6 | 13.5 |
| Raising contributions | – | 37.1 | 33.5 | 22.8 | 14.1 | 10.2 | 8.4 | 7.2 | 12.2 |
| More employees contribute | – | 2.8 | 2.8 | 2.4 | 1.0 | 0.2 | –0.2 | –0.3 | 0.5 |
| Survivors' pensions | – | 5.2 | 5.0 | 3.8 | 2.6 | 2.1 | 2.0 | 1.9 | 2.4 |

Sources: Ministry of Finance; and Fund staff estimates.

[1]Actuarial computations on the pension plans for teachers, public administration employees, army and police officers, university professors, and judges.
[2]NPV represents the net present value of operational balances between 2003 and 2050 at an annual real interest rate of 5 percent.
[3]Includes the effect of mandatory retirement (whenever applicable).

- In the short run, two measures, abolishing aguinaldo and raising the contribution rate, account for about two-thirds of the savings.[72] This is because these measures came into effect immediately with the approval of the reform and do not require time for their full effect to play out.

- In the long run, the bulk of savings—two-thirds of the net present value of savings between 2003 and 2050—arise from lowering the pension benefits. Lower pension benefits, in turn, are due to the joint effects of changing the replacement rates, the computation of the base wage, and the pension indexation mechanism. The effect of lowering pension benefits builds up slowly over time with the increase in the share of pensions regulated by the new regime, as current pension recipients die and are replaced by workers retiring under the new regime.

- Raising the retirement age has a positive effect on savings in the earlier years following the reform—it explains about one-fifth of total savings in 2004—but this effect declines over time and eventually turns negative, implying that raising the retirement age accounts for only 3 percent of savings in net present value terms.

---

[72]In 2004, these measures accounted for even more than implied by the findings in Table 3.10, since these do not take into account the transitory regime for teachers. Since this transitory regime reduces the savings from the teachers' plan, the relative importance of abolishing aguinaldo and raising the contribution rate is even greater.

## Box 3.2. Identifying the Sources of Savings of the Reform

In our calculations of the savings generated by the reform, we identified, for each pension plan, six distinct sources of savings (Table 3.10 reports the sum of the savings over the six underlying contributing plans). This box explains how we calculated each source of savings.

As regards the *disbursement* side, let $n$, $p$, and $m$ denote, for a given year, the number of pensions, the average monthly pension, and the number of months, respectively, in the prereform scenario; we use the same letters with a prime to denote the same variables in the postreform scenario during the same year. Total savings on the disbursement side can be decomposed as follows:

$$\text{Total savings from disbursement side} \equiv npm - n'p'm' = (n-n')pm + n'(p-p')m + n'p'(m-m').$$

The first term on the right-hand side represents the savings from raising the minimum retirement age at the old pension and without abolishing aguinaldo, since tighter age requirements tend to reduce the number of pension recipients in the postreform scenario relative to the prereform scenario, that is, $n-n'>0$. The second term represents the savings from lowering the pension benefits; because several measures introduced by the reform reduce the amount of pensions paid to the new and old pension recipients, $p-p'>0$. Finally, the third term represents the savings from abolishing aguinaldo, that is, $m-m'=1$.

As regards the *contribution* side, we used a similar approach to identify two sources of savings. Let $a$, $c$ and $m$ denote the number of active employees, the average monthly contribution by employee, and the number of months contributions are paid in the prereform scenario in a given year; as before, a prime denotes the same variables in the postreform scenario during the same year. Total savings from the contribution side can be decomposed as follows:

$$\text{Total savings from contribution side} \equiv a'c'm' - acm = (a'-a)cm + a'(c'-c)m.$$

The first term on the right-hand side represents the savings from raising the number of employees who contribute in the postreform scenario (owing to raising the minimum retirement age). The second term represents the savings from raising the average contribution (owing to raising the contribution rate from 14 to 16 percent). Finally, there is no effect from changing the number of months on the contribution side, as employees contribute the same number of months in the pre- and postreform scenario.

Finally, we included in Table 3.10 the savings from survivors' pensions. Under our simplifying assumptions, these result from three factors: the effect of the reform on the number of old-age pensions (since we kept the ratio of survivors' pensions to old-age pensions constant over time); the adjustment over time of survivors' pensions (based on wage increases in the prereform scenario and on CPI inflation in the postreform scenario); and the abolition of aguinaldo.

Mandatory retirement explains why raising the retirement age does not generate important savings in the long run. The reason for this is mandatory retirement, which the reform introduced as age 62 for public administration employees and judicial employees and as age 75 for university professors. Mandatory retirement *raises* over time the number of pension recipients in the postreform scenario relative to the prereform scenario because, when the population ages, forcing older workers to retire offsets the effect of raising the minimum retirement age. This offsetting occurs for public administration employees, university professors, and judicial employees (Figure 3.2), for whom the dependency ratios in the

## Figure 3.2. Dependency Ratios Before and After the Reform

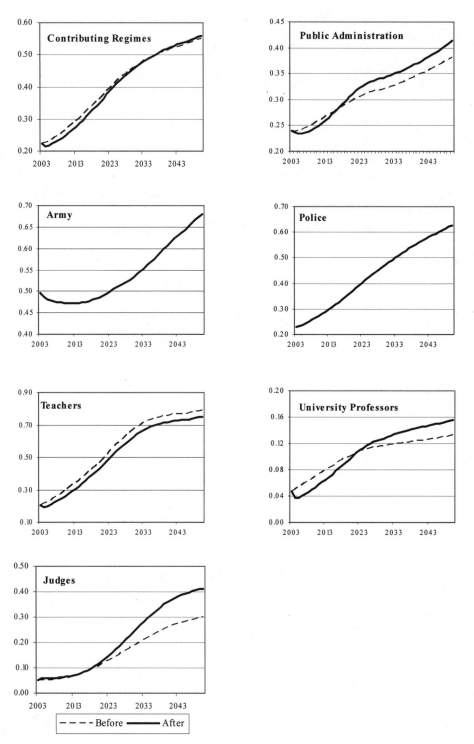

Sources: Ministry of Finance; and Fund staff estimates.

postreform scenario eventually exceed the dependency ratios in the prereform scenario. For the contributing plans as a whole, the implication is that, although the reform initially lowers the dependency ratio, eventually it has no effect.

## E. Assessment and Policy Implications

Our main conclusion is that, facing explosive dynamics, the reform generates major savings in net present value terms but leaves large unfunded liabilities. While bringing the caja fiscal into financial equilibrium may have been politically unrealistic, a net present value of deficits in the order of 45 percent of initial GDP in the postreform scenario will not be sustainable in the long run. As a result, further wide-ranging reforms will be required in the future to achieve long-term financial viability.

Decisive action will be required in the future to further tighten the minimum retirement age requirements. After the reform, the plans for teachers, the army, and police officers—the largest contributing plans—continue to generate very large net present values of deficits. These are also the plans for which the reform in minimum retirement ages was most timid, implying that for these plans the projected increase in dependency ratios is the highest among the contributing plans—the ratios for these plans stand above 0.6 in 2050. Future reform will have to address this shortcoming to counteract this rapid increase in dependency ratios and its effect on the deficits.

Mandatory requirement will also have to be reconsidered in the future. Apparently, the motivation for mandatory requirement was the desire to counteract a common practice of many older, low-productivity public employees to remain on the registry of active employees. However, mandatory requirement will interact with population aging in a perverse way, boosting dependency ratios and in turn operational deficits.

Chaco War pensions will require funding well into the future, albeit of declining size. By separating the administration of Chaco War pensions from the other contributing plans and by requesting that the former be fully funded in the annual budget law, the reform makes explicit the cost to society of Chaco War pensions. In this sense, earmarking specific tax revenues to the funding of Chaco War pensions would be highly desirable, since it would underscore the commitment of the Paraguayan society to its war heroes and their survivors.

While not considered in this chapter, efforts to purge the beneficiary rolls of false claims may generate important savings. Preliminary results achieved both in the context of contributing and noncontributing plans are particularly encouraging in terms of the savings that can be reaped through administrative improvements and the census of beneficiaries.

# References

Chand, Sheetal K., and Albert Jaeger, 1996, *Aging Population and Public Pension Schemes*, IMF Occasional Paper No. 147 (Washington: International Monetary Fund).

Oficina Internacional del Trabajo, 2003, *Paraguay: Evaluación Actuarial del Régimen de Jubilaciones y Pensiones Administrado por el Instituto de Previsión Social (IPS)* (Santiago).

World Bank, 2003, *Paraguay: Policy Options for the New Administration. Creating Conditions for Sustainable Growth* (Washington).

# 4 Equilibrium Real Exchange Rate in Paraguay

## A. Background

In recent years, Paraguay's real exchange rate has exhibited large fluctuations. From end-2000 through end-2002, a period characterized by subsequent banking crises and a deep recession, the real effective exchange rate shed about one-third of its value, which it recovered only slightly during 2003 and early 2004. Fluctuations in the real exchange rate were even larger in the earlier part of the 1980s. As shown in Figure 4.1, these fluctuations took place around a declining long-term trend.

As the economy emerges from its 2002 recession, the appropriate level of the real exchange rate is an overarching policy question. Besides affecting external competitiveness, the recent developments in the real exchange rate have complicated the conduct of monetary policy, as large inflows of official reserves have forced the Central Bank of Paraguay to issue—at a large quasi-fiscal cost—large amounts of debt paper to sterilize the impact of reserve accumulation on money growth. These developments in turn raise the question of whether the optimal policy is to allow a gradual real appreciation of the guaraní, which would be justified if the recent crises have left the guaraní undervalued in real terms. The answer to this question requires an assessment of the magnitude of the misalignment of the real exchange rate from its equilibrium value.

The purpose of this chapter is to estimate the long-term equilibrium real exchange rate at the end of 2003 and, as a result, the misalignment in the real exchange rate. We use a variety of potential explanatory variables for the equilibrium real exchange rate, which we define as the level toward which, absent new shocks, the real exchange rate converges in the long run. Our estimates of the misalignment vary somewhat across different empirical specifications, possibly owing to the short sample size. However, these estimates consistently show that the real exchange rate was undervalued at the end of 2003, by a magnitude ranging between 3 and 10 percent.

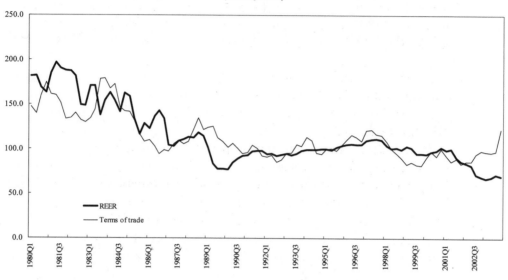

**Figure 4.1. Real Exchange Rate and Terms of Trade**
*(1995:Q1=100)*

Sources: International Monetary Fund; and Fund staff estimates.

The literature on estimating equilibrium real exchange rates is vast. Some recent papers that adopt the same methodology used in this chapter include Clark and MacDonald (2000), MacDonald and Ricci (2003), and Alberola, López, and Servén (2003). Readers are referred to these papers for thorough reviews of the theoretical and empirical literature.

The chapter is organized as follows. Section B briefly presents the empirical methodology that we use in this study. Section C presents our findings on the role of the terms of trade and regional factors using quarterly data. Section D performs some robustness exercises using annual data. Section E concludes.

## B. Empirical Methodology

We use co-integration techniques to identify a long-run co-integration relationship between the real effective exchange rate and its determinants.[73] As

---

[73]Using co-integration techniques is not the only possible approach, as determining the nonstationarity of macroeconomic time series in finite (and possibly very short) samples is difficult. On these grounds, Chen and Rogoff (2002) choose to work mainly with trend-stationary series. However, we take assurance from the large number of papers that conclude in favor of the existence of co-integration techniques among the real exchange rates and their determinants. For example, Cashin, Cespedes, and Sahay (2002) conclude that the real exchange rate and the commodity terms of trade are co-integrated in the case of Paraguay.

common in several other studies, we interpret this co-integration relationship as the long-run equilibrium relationship between the real exchange rate and its determinants (the "fundamentals"). We follow the methodology proposed by Johansen (1995) to investigate the existence of long-run co-integration relationships. This methodology is briefly described in this section.[74]

Our approach can be summarized as follows. We denote by $x_t$ the vector containing the real effective exchange rate and its determinants; the series in this vector are integrated of order one (denoted by I(1)). A co-integrating vector $b$ (of the same order as $x_t$) has the property that $bx_t$ is stationary, that is, integrated of order zero (I(0)). Intuitively, this property implies that any deviation from the long-run equilibrium is a stationary variable and therefore cannot diverge for too long from zero (or a constant value), that is, the variables in $x_t$ are nonstationary but tend to move "together" around an equilibrium relationship. Provided that the vector process $x_t$ admits a vector autoregression (VAR) representation, it can be reparameterized in terms of a vector error correction model (VECM) as follows:

$$\Delta x_t = \eta + \sum_{i=1}^{p} \Delta x_{t-i} + \Pi x_{t-1} + \varepsilon_t,$$

where $\Delta$ denotes the difference operator and $\eta$ and $\Pi$ are a vector and a matrix of parameters, respectively. By defining $\beta$, the matrix whose columns consist of all the linearly independent co-integration vectors, the VECM can be rewritten as

$$\Delta x_t = \eta + \sum_{i=1}^{p} \Delta x_{t-i} + \alpha\beta' x_{t-1} + \varepsilon_t,$$

where $\alpha$ is a matrix of adjustment coefficients, that is, the parameters that measure the speed at which the disequilibrium from the long-run equilibrium is eliminated (if the coefficients turn out to be negative).

We use standard tests to detect co-integration. Johansen (1995) provides two tests to detect the existence of co-integration relationships among the variables in $x_t$, the trace test and the maximum-eigenvalue test. In our study we employ these tests.

---

[74]See Clark and MacDonald (1998 and 2000) and MacDonald and Ricci (2003) for details.

## C. Role of Terms of Trade and Regional Factors

It is a well documented fact that, for commodity-producing countries, the terms of trade explain a large portion of the variation in the real effective exchange rate. This fact has recently been documented for industrial countries (Chen and Rogoff, 2002) and developing countries (Cashin, Cespedes, and Sahay, 2002).

Paraguay easily fits the definition of a commodity-producing economy. In fact, Paraguay stands out in Cashin, Cespedes, and Sahay's (2002) data set of 58 commodity-producing developing countries as one of the countries that can best be qualified as a "commodity currency," with three agricultural commodities—soybeans, cotton, and soy meals—accounting for about 80 percent of its exports.[75] Therefore, it is worth starting the analysis by investigating the relationship between the real exchange rate and the terms of trade.

It is reasonable to presume that an improvement in terms of trade would raise the real exchange rate. This is because, although the effect of terms of trade on the real exchange rate is ambiguous on theoretical grounds, an improvement in terms of trade would tend to increase domestic wages, and with them the demand for and the price of nontradable goods. Indeed, Cashin, Cespedes, and Sahay (2002) find that, for most countries in their sample, a rise in real commodity prices increases the long-run equilibrium real exchange rate. In particular, for the 22 countries for which they accept the null hypothesis of co-integration between the real exchange rate and the terms of trade, for only three do they estimate a negative elasticity of terms of trade on the real exchange rate; for the other countries, the estimated elasticity ranges between 0.2 and 2.

For the sake of comparability, we construct Paraguay's terms of trade index using the export shares provided by Cashin, Cespedes, and Sahay (2002). Following a common practice in this literature, we define the terms of trade as the weighted average of world commodity prices weighted by export shares, deflated by the world price of manufactured goods (proxied by the price of industrial country exports). This real price of commodities is more precisely described in the literature as "commodity terms of trade," but, for brevity, we will refer to it as "terms of trade." This definition ensures that the terms of trade are an exogenous variable from the perspective of Paraguay because it prevents changes in the nominal exchange rate from affecting the real exchange rate. Data sources and definitions are provided in the appendix to this chapter.

The strength of the positive co-movement between the real effective exchange rate and the terms of trade is striking in Paraguay (Figure 4.1). Nonetheless, the

---

[75]Out of 58 commodity-exporting countries, Paraguay is the seventh country in terms of share of commodity exports in total exports. Soybeans, cotton, and soy meals account for 44, 26, and 9 percent, respectively, of its exports.

figure also shows that the real exchange rate and the terms of trade can diverge for prolonged periods of time. In particular, this diverging behavior was observed starting from end-2001, when commodity prices began to rise sharply while the real exchange rate continued its downward movement as subsequent waves of crises hit Paraguay and the region.

The first part of this section investigates more formally the role of the terms of trade for the real exchange rate. Our sample consists initially of quarterly data covering 1980 through 2003. Although using quarterly data reduces the set of variables for which data are available, we begin our analysis with quarterly data to raise the number of observations used to estimate the dynamic structure of our empirical models. In Section D we perform some robustness exercises on these initial estimates using annual data.

### Test for nonstationarity

The preliminary requirement for co-integration that the univariate time series be integrated of order one is met. To test this property, Table 4.1 presents the Augmented Dickey-Fuller test and the Phillips-Perron test of the null hypothesis that the univariate time series are I(1). Both tests show the null hypothesis of unit roots in the real exchange rate (in logs) and the terms of trade (in logs) cannot be rejected. The two tests also do not reject the null hypothesis for Argentina's and Brazil's real effective exchange rates (in log), which we use below in our empirical analysis.

### Role of terms of trade

The simplest model relates the real exchange rate to the terms of trade. Column 1 in Table 4.2 presents selected results from estimating a vector error correction model on the real exchange rate and the terms of trade. We find that a high number of lags (11) are required to eliminate serial correlation from the residuals.[76] The trace test shows that we cannot reject, at the 5 percent confidence level, the null hypothesis that there is one co-integration relationship between the real exchange rate and the terms of trade (both in logs).

The long-run elasticity of the real exchange rate with respect to the terms of trade is high but reasonable. While high, 1.4, it is not out of line with the estimate for Paraguay reported by Cashin, Cespedes, and Sahay (2002), 0.99, which is itself

---

[76]Although this number could be reduced further by dropping recursively insignificant lags from the VECM, we maintain 11 lags to ensure that the residuals do not display any significant autocorrelations. We also include centered seasonal dummies.

## Table 4.1. Unit Root Tests

| | Augmented Dickey-Fuller[1] | | | | Phillips-Perron[1] | | |
|---|---|---|---|---|---|---|---|
| | t-stat | p-value[2] | Lag length[3] | DW statistic | Adj. t-stat | p-value[2] | Band-width[4] |
| Real effective exchange rate (log) | | | | | | | |
| Paraguay | −1.225 | 0.66 | 5 | 1.82 | −1.204 | 0.67 | 8 |
| Argentina | −1.805 | 0.37 | 0 | 1.87 | −1.940 | 0.31 | 2 |
| Brazil | −1.780 | 0.38 | 0 | 1.93 | −1.855 | 0.35 | 2 |
| Terms of trade (log) | −2.036 | 0.27 | 0 | 1.64 | −2.201 | 0.20 | 4 |

Sources: International Monetary Fund; and Fund staff estimates.

[1]Null hypothesis is that the series has a unit root.
[2]One-sided p-values.
[3]Automatic based on SIC (Schwartz information criterion).
[4]Newey-West using Bartlett kernel.

one of the highest estimates for commodity-producing countries. The estimated adjustment coefficient shows that the adjustment toward the long-term equilibrium is quite rapid, 20 percent per quarter, implying that the half-life of the adjustment to the long-run equilibrium is just over three quarters. This estimate is reasonable and compares with the estimates reported by Cashin, Cespedes, and Sahay (2002), who find that the median half-life for commodity-producing countries is eight months.

However, the evidence of co-integration is not unquestionably strong, possibly because other variables that affect the long-term equilibrium real exchange rate have been omitted from the empirical relationship. Unit root tests on the residuals from regressing the real exchange rate on the terms of trade (in logs) support this interpretation, as the null of a unit root in the residuals cannot be rejected.[77] This suggests that some persistent real exchange rate determinant may have been omitted, a problem that Chen and Rogoff (2002) also find and refer to as "nagging persistence."

### Role of regional factors

For a small economy such as Paraguay's, regional factors are natural first candidates as additional determinants of the real exchange rate. A simple way to

---

[77]A word of caution: this test on the residuals is not conclusive, as its distribution is not entirely correct when the test is performed on residuals from a first-stage regression.

## Table 4.2. Selected Results from VECM Estimation
### (*Quarterly data*)

|  |  | (1) | (2) | (3) | (4) |
|---|---|---|---|---|---|
| Number of co-integrating vectors |  |  |  |  |  |
| Trace test | 5 percent | 1 | 1 | 2 | 2 |
|  | 1 percent | 0 | 1 | 2 | 2 |
| Max-eigenvalue test | 5 percent | 0 | 1 | 2 | 2 |
|  | 1 percent | 0 | 0 | 1 | 2 |
| Co-integration vector[1] |  |  |  |  |  |
| REER (–1) |  | 1 | 1 | 1 | 1 |
| TOT (–1) |  | –1.40 | –1.37 | –1.99 | –4.76 |
|  |  | (0.16) | (0.19) | (–0.17) | (1.61) |
| REER Brazil (–1) |  | . . . | –0.53 |  | 13.1 |
|  |  | . . . | (0.28) |  | (1.8) |
| REER Argentina (–1) |  |  |  | –0.42 | –5.12 |
|  |  |  | . . . | (0.1) | (1.16) |
| Adjustment coefficient[2] |  | –0.20 | –0.18 | –0.17 | 0.003 |
|  |  | (0.08) | (0.06) | (0.08) | (0.008) |
| Lags in VECM[3] |  | 11 | 11 | 11 | 11 |
| N (after adjusting for endpoints) |  | 84 | 84 | 84 | 84 |

Sources: International Monetary Fund; and Fund staff estimates.

[1]Standard errors in parentheses.
[2]Coefficient on the co-integrating equation in the ECM representation for Paraguay's log real effective exchange rate.
[3]Number of lags in first differences in VECM representation.

take regional factors into account is to include the real effective exchange rates of the two largest economies in the region which are Paraguay's main trading partners, Argentina and Brazil. Besides cyclical conditions, real exchange rates in the neighboring economies could indirectly capture the effect of productivity developments in the region on the real exchange rate—under the assumption that productivity in Paraguay reflects to some extent productivity in its large neighboring countries. Figure 4.2 shows that indeed the real exchange rates of Paraguay, Argentina, and Brazil tend to move closely together.

101

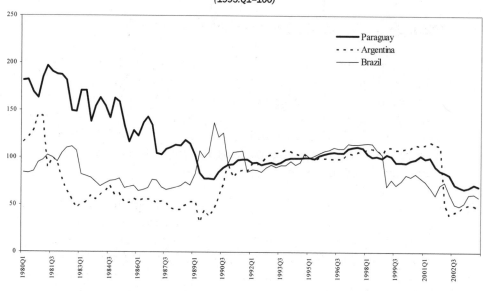

Figure 4.2. Real Effective Exchange Rates for Paraguay, Argentina, and Brazil
(1995:Q1=100)

Sources: International Monetary Fund; and Fund staff estimates.

We find stronger evidence of co-integration when we add Brazil's real effective exchange to our empirical specification (Table 4.2, column 2). The estimates of the long-run effect of terms of trade on Paraguay's real exchange rate are similar to our previous estimates. However, we find that Brazil's real exchange rate also has a strong and statistically significant long-run effect on Paraguay's real exchange rate. The estimate in column 2 shows that a 1 percent depreciation in Brazil's real effective exchange rate causes a real effective depreciation in the guaraní of 0.5 percent. The adjustment to the long-run equilibrium also remains similar to our previous estimate (implying a half-life of the disequilibrium of 3.5 quarters).

We find similar results using Argentina's real exchange rate (Table 4.2, column 3). The co-integration tests indicate a second co-integration relation (not reported in the table), whose coefficients, however, do not appear reasonable on economic grounds. The estimate of the effect of the terms of trade is higher (close to 2), and Argentina's real exchange rate is found to have a strong long-run effect on Paraguay's real exchange rate (the elasticity is about 0.4).

We do not find sensible results when we use both Brazil's and Argentina's real exchange rates (Table 4.2, column 4). Using both Argentina's and Brazil's real exchange rates together with the terms of trade does not yield sensible results in terms of the magnitude and sign of the coefficients in the long-run relationship and in the adjustment coefficient—the latter is positive but not statistically

102

significant—possibly reflecting multicolinearity between Brazil's and Argentina's real exchange rates.

## Misalignment from long-run equilibrium

We use the previous estimates for a first assessment of the misalignment in Paraguay's real effective exchange rate at the end of 2003. The results from the empirical model with the terms of trade only and the models that add Brazil's and Argentina's real effective exchange rate in turn (corresponding to columns 1–3 in Table 4.2) are plotted in Figure 4.3. In each panel, we compute Paraguay's long-run real effective exchange using the coefficients from the co-integration vectors reported in columns 1–3 of Table 4.2.

As a preliminary step, we need to compute the long-run values of the determinants of the real exchange rate. This is because, to compute the long-run equilibrium real exchange rate, we need to evaluate the co-integration relationship using the long-run equilibrium values for the determinants of Paraguay's real exchange rate, that is, the terms of trade and the real exchange rates of Brazil and Argentina. More precisely, denoting by $b$ the long-run coefficients on the determinants of the real exchange rate[78] and by $\hat{f}$ the long-run values of the fundamental determinants of the real exchange rate, we define the long-run equilibrium real exchange rate as $b\hat{f}$. To compute the long-run value of the fundamentals, we follow the simple approach suggested by MacDonald and Ricci (2003) of smoothing the real exchange rate determinants with the Hodrick-Prescott filter.[79]

This method of defining long-run values of the fundamentals has shortcomings. The main limitation is likely to be that, being completely statistical in nature, this method is sensitive to persistent departures of the smoothed series from their long-run equilibrium values, because the filter tends to interpret these departures as shifts in the long-run trends. This problem is likely to be particularly severe when smoothing the real exchange rate of the neighboring economies, since real exchange rates are known to exhibit long-lasting departures from their equilibrium values. For example, Alberola, López, and Servén (2003) show that the Argentine peso underwent a prolonged and growing real appreciation away from its long-term equilibrium during the second part of the 1990s through the end of 2001.

---

[78]These coefficients are obtained by changing the sign of the parameters in the co-integration vector.

[79]We use the smoothing factor of 1,600, the recommended factor for quarterly data.

## Figure 4.3. Actual and Long-Run Equilibrium Real Effective Exchange Rate

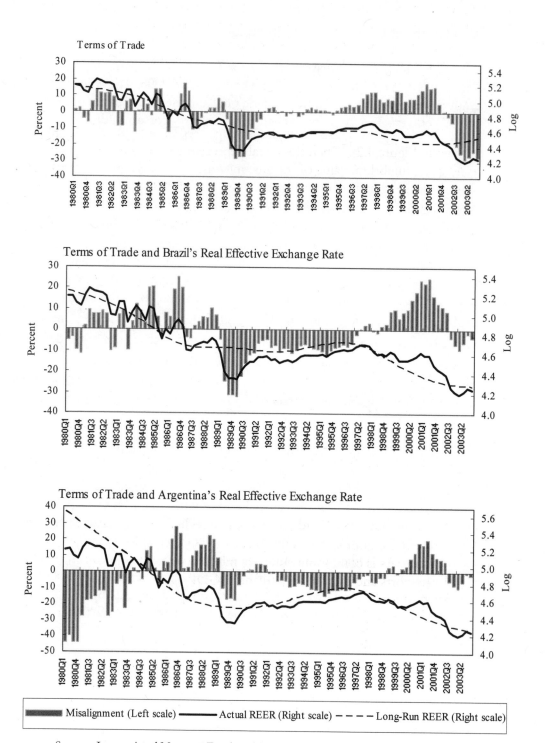

Sources: International Monetary Fund; and Fund staff estimates.

When computing the end-2003 misalignment, it is critical to control for regional factors (Figure 4.3). The top panel, based on the model with terms of trade only, shows that the drop in the real value of the guaraní starting from the beginning of 2002 produced a widening misalignment in the actual real exchange rate from its long-run equilibrium value, as the latter increased as a result of the ongoing improvement in the terms of trade (as shown in Figure 4.1). According to this first model, at the end of 2003 the real effective exchange rate was undervalued by about 27 percent. However, this model, by including the terms of trade only, does not take into account the developments in the neighboring countries, which were simultaneously experiencing a rapid real depreciation in their currencies (as shown in Figure 4.2). When these real depreciations are taken into account, the long-run equilibrium value of the guaraní continued to *decline* after 2001, implying that the undervaluation in real terms at the end of 2003 was much smaller, 3 and 2 percent using the model with Brazil's and Argentina's real effective exchange rates, respectively (as shown in the second and third panel of Figure 4.3).

## D. Robustness

To check the robustness of the previous results, we turn to annual data. A larger set of variables is available at the annual frequency. However, the drawback of using annual data is that the number of observations falls dramatically.

Besides terms of trade and regional factors, some common determinants considered in the literature are the following:[80]

- Productivity differentials (the Balassa-Samuelson effect). An increase in productivity (relative to trading partners) in tradable goods raises the relative price of nontradable goods and thus raises the real exchange rate. We measure this effect by introducing real per capita GDP relative to the United States' real per capita GDP.

- Trade openness. A more open trade regime increases competition in tradable goods, reducing their price and thus lowering the real exchange rate. As is commonly done, we measure trade openness as the sum of exports and imports in percent of GDP.

- Fiscal balance. An improvement in fiscal balance tends to reduce the demand for nontradable goods and thus lower the real exchange rate. We measure the fiscal balance as central government balance in percent of GDP.

---

[80]This discussion follows MacDonald and Ricci (2003), who provide further references to theoretical papers underpinning these channels.

- Current account balance. By definition, the current account balance determines the change in a country's stock of net foreign assets. Thus, an increase in capital inflows that is reflected in a worsening current account balance may cause an appreciation of the real exchange rate as demand for nontradables increases.[81] We measure the current account balance in percent of GDP.

- Net foreign assets. Higher net foreign assets allow a higher level of consumption and therefore tend to raise the price of nontradable goods and the real exchange rate. We measure net foreign assets as the sum of official reserves and the banking system's foreign assets in percent of GDP.

Figure 4.4 plots these potential determinants of the real effective exchange rates, together with the annual series of the terms of trade and the real exchange rates of Brazil and Argentina.[82]

## Least-square estimates of long-run equilibrium

We start by estimating the long-run equilibrium relationship directly (Table 4.3). As the reason for this is that the number of observations falls sharply with annual data (we have 24 annual observations in our sample), it is convenient to estimate the long-run equilibrium relationships directly by regressing Paraguay's real exchange rate on its determinants.[83]

We first replicate the results found on quarterly data (Table 4.3, columns 1–3). Table 4.3 reports the regressions corresponding to the VECM representations estimated on quarterly data (reported in columns 1–3 of Table 4.1). The terms of trade and the real exchange rates of the neighboring countries explain about two-thirds of the annual variation in Paraguay's real exchange rate over 1980–2003. While roughly in line with the co-integration vectors reported in Table 4.2, the coefficients on the terms of trade and Brazil's and Argentina's real effective exchange rates are somewhat smaller. The low values of the Durbin-Watson statistics show that the residuals exhibit some serial correlation, indicating that other relevant variables may have been omitted from these specifications.

---

[81]However, the negative association between the current account balance and the real exchange rate may simply reflect reverse causality, as a lower real exchange rate may stimulate more exports and discourage imports.

[82]For some series we also plot the Hodrick-Prescott trend (using a smoothing factor of 100).

[83]If the variables included in the regression are co-integrated, the least-square estimates are "super-consistent." However, the least-square standard errors are not correct, since they need to be corrected for the nonstandard distribution of the estimator in the presence of nonstationary time series. A procedure that corrects for this problem, the dynamic least squares proposed by Stock and Watson (1993), requires introducing leads and lags of the right-hand side variables, further reducing the size of the sample available for estimation.

## Figure 4.4. Determinants of the Real Effective Exchange Rate, 1980–2003

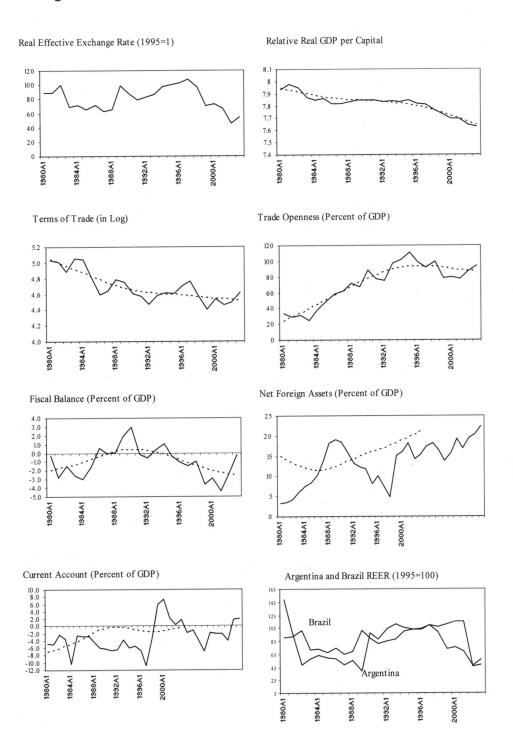

Sources: International Monetary Fund; and Fund staff estimates.

### Table 4.3. Least-Square Estimates of Long-Run Equilibrium

| | Dependent variable: REER | | | | |
| --- | --- | --- | --- | --- | --- |
| | (1) | (2) | (3) | (4) | (5) |
| Terms of trade (log) | 1.11*** | 1.09*** | 1.17*** | 0.31** | 0.22 |
| | (0.17) | (0.18) | (0.17) | (0.14) | (0.14) |
| REER Brazil | | 0.11 | | 0.003 | 0.2 |
| | | (0.17) | | (0.13) | (0.18) |
| REER Argentina | | | 0.14* | 0.1 | 0.06 |
| | | | (0.08) | (0.06) | (0.05) |
| Current account balance | | | | −0.016*** | −0.014** |
| | | | | (0.01) | (0.01) |
| Fiscal balance | | | | −0.018 | −0.054** |
| | | | | (0.01) | (0.02) |
| Foreign assets | | | | −0.001** | 0.005 |
| | | | | (0.01) | (0.00) |
| Openness | | | | −0.003** | 0.001 |
| | | | | (0.00) | (0.00) |
| Relative GDP per capita | | | | 1.12** | −0.60 |
| | | | | (0.48) | (1.15) |
| Linear trend | | | | | −0.037** |
| | | | | | (0.02) |
| Constant | −0.52 | −0.87 | −1.40 | −5.77 | 7.44 |
| | (0.80) | (0.97) | (0.92) | (3.29) | (8.48) |
| R-squared | 0.66 | 0.66 | 0.7 | 0.95 | 0.96 |
| Adjusted R-squared | 0.64 | 0.63 | 0.67 | 0.93 | 0.94 |
| Durbin-Watson stat | 0.99 | 1.01 | 1.09 | 2.76 | 2.85 |
| N | 24 | 24 | 24 | 24 | 24 |

Sources: International Monetary Fund; and Fund staff estimates.

Standard errors in parentheses (not corrected for co-integration) in columns. Newey-West heteroscedasticity and autocorrelation consistent (HAC) standard errors in column 5.

*, Denotes significance at the 10 percent level; **, at the 5 percent level; and ***, at the 1 percent level.

From a general specification that includes other potential explanatory variables we find the following results (Table 4.3, column 4):

- The coefficient on the terms of trade remains positive but falls sharply when more fundamentals are included in the equation—the elasticity of the real exchange rate is 0.3—and continues to be statistically significant at the 5 percent confidence level.[84]

---

[84]As remarked in the previous footnotes, statements about the statistical significance have to be handled with care, since the standard errors in columns 1–4 are not corrected for the nonstationarity of the included variables.

- The real effective exchange rates for Brazil and Argentina are no longer significant, indicating that in the previous regressions they may have proxied for other omitted variables. In particular, they may have proxied for the long-term decline in relative productivity, the Balassa-Samuelson effect, picked up by relative GDP per capita. As expected from inspecting Figure 4.4, this has a large positive coefficient that implies that a 1 percent fall in GDP per capita lowers the real effective exchange rate by about 1 percent.

- The current account balance has a negative small coefficient. As noted above, the negative sign may reflect reverse causality, that is, the fact that a rise in the real exchange rate causes a worsening in the current account balance by negatively affecting competitiveness and net exports.

- As expected, the fiscal balance has a negative sign, indicating that an increase in fiscal deficit by 1 percent of GDP appreciates the real exchange rate by about 2 percent. This effect is not statistically significant, however.

- Trade openness has a small negative effect on the real exchange rate, showing that trade openness works as a tariff: an increase in external competition tends to lower the price of tradable goods and thus the real exchange rate.

- Foreign assets do not have a quantitatively nor statistically significant effect. This finding is not surprising, given the small role of capital account transactions in Paraguay. This contrasts, for example, with the important role of net foreign assets found for emerging market economies such as Argentina (Alberola, López, and Servén, 2003) and South Africa (MacDonald and Ricci, 2003).

We find that our results are broadly robust to the introduction of a linear time trend (Table 4.3, column 5). This is the specification estimated that would be appropriate if the data were trend-stationary. The estimates in column 5 remain broadly in line with those in column 4. The coefficient on terms of trade falls relative to column 4 (to 0.22) and is not significant at the 10 percent confidence level (its p-value is 0.14). The real exchange rates of Brazil and Argentina continue to be statistically insignificant, and the coefficient on the current account and fiscal balances remain negative—both are now statistically significant at the 5 percent level. The main difference with the specification in column 4 is the role of relative GDP per capita, which has now a negative (but statistically insignificant) coefficient. This difference is not surprising, given that the long-term decline in productivity is now captured by the linear trend, which indicates that over the sample period the real exchange rate has declined on average by almost 4 percent a year.[85]

The general model implies that the real exchange rate was undervalued in 2003. Figure 4.5 provides a visual summary of the goodness of fit of the general model estimated in column 4. The residuals from this model (based on the actual values of the explanatory variables) indicate that in 2003 Paraguay's real exchange rate was undervalued by about 3 percent, an estimate that is close to the estimates found in the previous section. The figure also plots the misalignment from the long-run real effective exchange rate computed by smoothing the determinants of the real exchange rate with the Hodrick-Prescott filter (using a factor of 100). According to this estimate, the misalignment for 2003 is higher, about 15 percent.

It is useful to investigate the sources of this undervaluation (Table 4.4). Using the estimates of our general specification (column 4 of Table 4.3), Table 4.4 breaks down the misalignment into the portion that is accounted by the misalignment of the fundamentals from their long-run trend and the portion that cannot be explained by observed variables (this latter portion corresponds to the estimated regression residual for 2003). When we evaluate the fundamentals at their actual 2003 values, the real exchange rate turns out to be 2.6 percent undervalued (this misalignment is plotted as the residual in Figure 4.5). However, when we adjust the fundamentals to their long-run values (defined as their Hodrick-Prescott trends), the misalignment rises to 15 percent. This is because the estimate of the equilibrium real exchange rate is 12.5 percent higher—and as a result the undervaluation is higher—when all the fundamentals are evaluated at their long-run values rather than at their actual values. More specifically:

- Adjusting the current account balance to its trend value in 2003 (lower than its actual value) *raises* the equilibrium real exchange rate by 4 percent.

- Adjusting the fiscal balance to its trend value in 2003 (lower than its actual value) *raises* the equilibrium real exchange by 4 percent.

- Adjusting Argentina's real exchange rate to its trend value in 2003 (higher than its actual value) *raises* the equilibrium real exchange rate by 3 percent.

---

[85]A simple regression of relative per capita GDP on a linear trend shows that relative GDP per capita has fallen on average by 1 percent a year over our sample period. The trend accounts for almost 80 percent of the variation in relative GDP per capita.

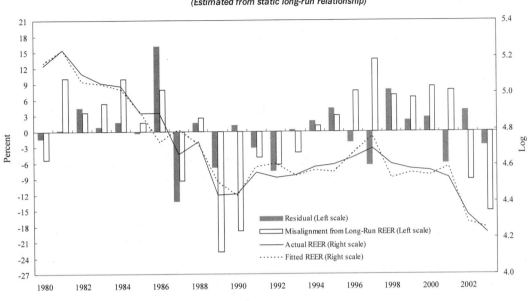

**Figure 4.5. Fitted Real Exchange Rate and Misalignment from Long-Run Equilibrium**
*(Estimated from static long-run relationship)*

Source: International Monetary Fund; and Fund staff estimates.

- Adjusting the terms of trade to their trend value in 2003 (lower than their actual value) *lowers* the equilibrium real exchange rate by 3 percent.

- Adjusting openness to its trend value in 2003 (lower than its actual value) *raises* the equilibrium real exchange rate by 2 percent.

- Adjusting relative real GDP per capita to its trend value in 2003 (higher than its actual value) raises the equilibrium real exchange rate by 1.5 percent.

- Adjusting net foreign assets and Brazil's real exchange rate at their trend values does not have any quantitatively relevant effect on the equilibrium real exchange rate.

Our method of computing long-run values for the fundamentals tends to overestimate the misalignment in 2003. This is because the Hodrick-Prescott filter, which is used to compute the long-run fundamental values, may fail to capture important developments that occurred at the end of our sample period,[86] a point that is particularly relevant when computing the long-run fiscal balance.

---

[86]This is the well-known end-point problem of the Hodrick-Prescott filter.

### Table 4.4. Breakdown of Misalignment in 2003
*(In percent of long-run equilibrium)[1]*

| | |
|---|---|
| Misalignment[2] | −15.1 |
| Accounted by fundamentals[3] | −12.5 |
|     Current account | −4.1 |
|     Fiscal balance | −4.3 |
|     REER Argentina | −3.4 |
|     REER Brazil | 0.0 |
|     Terms of trade | 3.1 |
|     Net Foreign Assets | −0.1 |
|     Openness | −2.2 |
|     Relative GDP per capita | −1.5 |
| Unaccounted by fundamentals[4] | −2.6 |

[1]Based on the estimates of the general model in column 4 of Table 4.3.
[2]Difference between actual REER and long-run equilibrium. The latter is computed by evaluating the regression in column 4 of Table 4.3 at the long-run value of the fundamentals (according to the HP filter).
[3]Difference between actual and long-term value of the fundamental (according to the HP trend) multiplied by respective coefficient in column 4 of Table 4.3.
[4]Residual for 2003 (in percent of long-run trend).

The large fiscal deficits prior to 2003 imply that the long-run fiscal balance for 2003 computed using the Hodrick-Prescott filter is also large. However, this procedure ignores that Paraguay's new government started an ambitious fiscal consolidation program in the second half of 2003. If the fiscal balance for 2003 is considered to be more indicative of the trend in government finances than the recent past (as it seems likely), then the misalignment of the real exchange rate implied by the fiscal balance is much smaller, bringing down the overall real misalignment toward 10 percent.

Conversely, other factors could raise the long-run value of the real exchange rate in the near future. In the short run, the most important factor in this sense is related to the size of the current real underappreciation of the Argentine peso. If the long-term real value of the Argentine peso were even higher than implied by the Hodrick-Prescott trend (because its value at end-2003 is excessively sensitive to the large 2001 depreciation), then the long-run value of the guaraní would be higher, and with it the resulting estimated misalignment.[87] Similarly, if the recent increase in terms of trade proved to be persistent, the long-run value of the guaraní would be higher.[88] Finally, if sustained growth were to return to Paraguay, raising relative per capita GDP, the long-run value of the guaraní would also be higher.

---

[87]According to the Hodrick-Prescott filter, in 2003 the Argentine peso was 35 percent below its trend value.

[88]However, the latest *World Economic Outlook* projections suggest that the current upturn in terms of trade may not be a long-term phenomenon.

## Error correction models

To check robustness, we also estimate error correction models on annual data (Table 4.5). The small number of observations constrains the dynamic structure of the models that we can estimate. As a result, we start with small models (which allow for some dynamics) and we add potentially omitted variables in light of the previous results.

We find evidence of co-integration in most specifications. We find some evidence of co-integration in all but the specification that includes the terms of trade and Brazil's real exchange rate as determinants of the real exchange rate (column 2). For some specifications the co-integration tests show that we cannot reject the presence of more co-integration relationships (we report only the first one). The half-life of the misalignment from the long-run equilibrium implied by the adjustment coefficients range between 6 (column 2) and 9 months (column 4) and are roughly in line with the findings on quarterly data (ranging from 9 to 12 months). Only in the specification in column 5 does the adjustment coefficient turn out positive (but statistically insignificant). The estimates of the coefficients on terms of trade in the co-integration relationships across the various relationships are also in line with the findings on quarterly data and from estimating the long-run relationship directly, except in columns 5 and 6, for which the estimates are slightly lower.

We also broadly replicate our earlier results found on quarterly data. With regard to the models that were also estimated on quarterly data, the co-integration equations for the models with the terms of trade only and with the real exchange rates for Brazil and Argentina (columns 1–3) replicate well the findings on quarterly data (columns 1–3 of Table 4.2). In column 4, we replace relative per capita GDP (as a proxy for the Balassa-Samuelson effect) to Brazil's and Argentina's real exchange rates as a measure of productivity pressures on the real exchange rate. As in the long-run equation presented in Table 4.4, we find that relative per capita GDP has a quantitatively strong long-run effect on the real exchange rate, since a 1 percent fall in relative GDP per capita lowers the real exchange rate by 1 percent.[89] In column 5 of Table 4.5 we add current account balance and the fiscal balance (in percent of GDP) to the specification in column 4 and we find effects similar to what was previously found for the long-run relationship (column 4 of Table 4.3). In particular, worsening the current account balance or the fiscal balance raises the real exchange rate.[90] Column 6 of Table 4.5 presents the most general error correction model (ECM) representation, corresponding to the most general specification for the long-run relationship in column 4 of Table 4.3, except for the exclusion of Brazil's and Argentina's real

---

[89]The estimated coefficient is close to being significant at the 5 percent significance level.

[90]However, the "wrong" positive sign of the adjustment coefficient suggests that this model is not well specified.

### Table 4.5. Selected Results from VECM estimation
*(Annual data)*

| | | (1) | (2) | (3) | (4) | (5) | (6) |
|---|---|---|---|---|---|---|---|
| Number of co-integrating vectors | | | | | | | |
| Trace test | 5 percent | 1 | 0 | 3 | 2 | 2 | 0 |
| | 1 percent | 0 | 0 | 3 | 1 | 2 | 0 |
| Max-eigenvalue test | 5 percent | 1 | 0 | 3 | 2 | 0 | 1 |
| | 1 percent | 0 | 0 | 1 | 0 | 0 | 0 |
| Co-integration vector[1] | | | | | | | |
| REER (–1) | | 1 | 1 | 1 | 1 | 1 | 1 |
| TOT (–1) | | –1.37 | –1.33 | –1.86 | –0.91 | –0.55 | –0.22 |
| | | (0.13) | (0.14) | (0.11) | (0.27) | (0.13) | (0.06) |
| REER Brazil (–1) | | | –0.12 | | | | |
| | | | (0.22) | | | | |
| REER Argentina (–1) | | | | –0.37 | | | |
| | | | | (0.08) | | | |
| Relative per capita GDP | | | | | –1.02 | –1.61 | –1.47 |
| | | | | | (0.65) | (0.35) | (0.15) |
| Current account | | | | | | 0.02 | 0.02 |
| | | | | | | (0.00) | (0.00) |
| Fiscal balance | | | | | | 0.08 | 0.04 |
| | | | | | | (0.01) | (0.00) |
| Openness | | | | | | | 0.004 |
| | | | | | | | (0.000) |
| Adjustment coefficient[2] | | –0.62 | –0.49 | –0.52 | –0.74 | 0.47 | –0.14 |
| | | (0.24) | (0.19) | (0.17) | (0.21) | (0.33) | (0.33) |
| Lags in VECM[3] | | 2 | 2 | 2 | 2 | 1 | 0 |
| N (after adjusting for endpoints) | | 21 | 21 | 21 | 21 | 22 | 23 |

Sources: International Monetary Fund; and Fund staff estimates.

[1]Standard errors in parentheses.
[2]Coefficient on co-integrating equation in the ECM representation for Paraguay's log real effective exchange rate.
[3]Number of lags in first differences in VECM representation.

exchange rates and net foreign assets (which were found to play a negligible role).[91] All the estimates have values in line with the previous findings.

The estimated misalignment in the real exchange rate in 2003 is also consistent with previous findings. The general model in column 6 implies that when all the determinants of the real exchange rate are evaluated at their long-run equilibrium (according to the Hodrick-Prescott filter), the real exchange rate in 2003 was about 17 percent below its long-run equilibrium (Figure 4.6). Deviations of the

[91]This specification could be estimated only after eliminating all the lags on differenced variables.

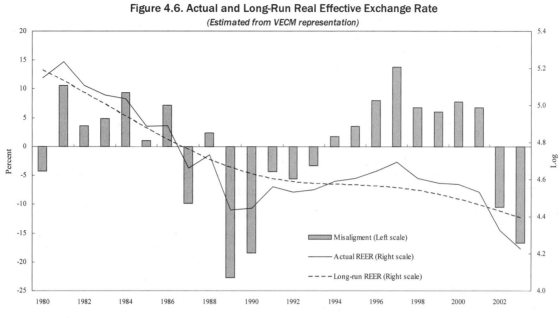

**Figure 4.6. Actual and Long-Run Real Effective Exchange Rate**
*(Estimated from VECM representation)*

Sources: International Monetary Fund; and Fund staff estimates.

fundamentals from their long-term values account for 14 percent of this misalignment, with the fiscal balance in turn accounting for more than half of this. This implies that if the fiscal balance in 2003 were regarded as a long-term measure of fiscal policy, the misalignment would fall below 10 percent.[92]

## E. Conclusions

Our estimates showed a real undervaluation in the guaraní at the end of 2003 in the range of 3–10 percent. We estimated several empirical models and found a range of estimates of the real misalignment in the guaraní at the end of 2003. Although these estimates are consistent in pointing out an underappreciation in real terms, the range of the estimated misalignment is relatively large, between 3 to 15 percent, possibly as a consequence of the small size of our sample. However, we argued that we can narrow this range to 3–10 percent once we take into account the fiscal consolidation that was started by the new government in the second half of 2003.

---

[92]The same caveat with regard to the long-term values of the terms of trade and relative per capita GDP applies in this context.

Other factors could, in the near future, raise the long-run value of the real exchange rate and thus the size of the misalignment. In the short run, the most important factor in this sense could be the magnitude of the current underappreciation in real terms of the Argentine peso, whose recovery could pull up the long-term equilibrium value of the guaraní. Similarly, persistently high commodity prices and the return of sustained growth to Paraguay would raise the long-term real value of the guaraní, raising in turn the magnitude of the misalignment in 2003.

# References

Alberola, Enrique, Humberto López, and Luis Servén, 2003, "Tango with the Gringo: The Hard Peg and Real Misalignment in Argentina" (unpublished; Washington: World Bank).

Cashin, Paul A., Luis Cespedes, and Ratna Sahay, 2002, "Keynes, Cocoa, and Copper: In Search of Commodity Currencies," IMF Working Paper 02/223 (Washington: International Monetary Fund).

Chen, Yu-chin, and Kenneth Rogoff, 2002, "Commodity Currencies and Empirical Exchange Rate Puzzles," IMF Working Paper 02/27 (Washington: International Monetary Fund).

Clark, Peter B., and Ronald MacDonald, 1998, "Exchange Rates and Economic Fundamentals—A Methodological Comparison of BEERs and FEERs," IMF Working Paper 98/67 (Washington: International Monetary Fund).

———, 2000, "Filtering the BEER—A Permanent and Transitory Decomposition," IMF Working Paper 00/144 (Washington: International Monetary Fund).

Johansen, Soren, 1995, *Likelihood-Based Inference in Cointegrated Autoregressive Vectors* (Oxford: Oxford University Press).

MacDonald, Ronald, and Luca A. Ricci, 2003, "Estimation of the Equilibrium Real Exchange Rate for South Africa," IMF Working Paper 03/44 (Washington: International Monetary Fund).

Stock, James, and Mark Watson, 1993, "A Simple Estimator of Cointegrating Vectors in Higher Order Integrated Systems," *Econometrica*, Vol. 61, No. 4, pp. 783–820.

# Appendix 1. Data Sources and Definitions

| Variable | Source | Code | Comment |
|---|---|---|---|
| Paraguay real effective exchange rate | *International Financial Statistics* | 288..RECZF... | Real effective exchange rate based on relative consumer prices (normalized to 1995=100 for annual data and 1995:Q1 for quarterly data). |
| Cotton price index | *International Financial Statistics* | 11176F.DZFM40 | |
| Soybean price index | *International Financial Statistics* | 11176JFDZF | |
| Soybean meal price index | *International Financial Statistics* | 11176JJDZF... | |
| Industrial countries export price index | *International Financial Statistics* | 11074..DZF... | |
| Paraguay export price index | — | — | Weighted average of soybean, cotton and soybean meal price indexes using shares of 44, 26, and 9, respectively (provided by Cashin, Cespedes, and Sahay (2002)). |
| Paraguay terms of trade | — | — | Computed by dividing Paraguay export price by industrial countries export price (normalized to 1995=100 for annual data and 1995:Q1=100 for quarterly data). |
| Argentina real effective exchange rate | *Information Notice System* | I213EREER | Real effective exchange rate based on relative consumer prices (normalized to 1995=100 for annual data and 1995:Q1 for quarterly data) |
| Brazil real effective exchange rate | *Information Notice System* | I223EREER | Real effective exchange rate based on relative consumer prices (normalized to 1995=100 for annual data and 1995:Q1 for quarterly data). |
| Paraguay GDP at current prices | *World Economic Outlook* | W288NGDP | |
| Paraguay GDP at constant prices | *World Economic Outlook* | W288NGDP_R | |
| Paraguay real GDP per capita | *World Economic Outlook* | W288NGDPRPC | |
| United States real GDP per capita | *World Economic Outlook* | W111NGDPRPC | |
| Relative GDP per capita | — | — | Log difference between Paraguay real GDP per capita and United States GDP per capita. |
| Current account balance | *World Economic Outlook* | W288BCA | |
| Imports of goods and services | *World Economic Outlook* | W288BM | |
| Exports of goods and services | *World Economic Outlook* | W288BX | |
| Central government fiscal balance | *World Economic Outlook* | W288GCB | Used in percent of GDP. |
| Trade openness | — | — | Sum of imports and exports in percent of GDP. |
| Net international reserves | *International Financial Statistics* | 28811...ZF... | |
| Bank foreign assets | *International Financial Statistics* | 28821...ZF... | |
| Net foreign assets | — | — | Sum of net international reserves and bank foreign assets in percent of GDP. |